PENN & TELLER'S
How To Play
With Your Food

PENN & TELLER'S
HOW TO PLAY WITH YOUR FOOD

BY

PENN JILLETTE AND TELLER

PHOTOGRAPHS BY ANTHONY LOEW / DESIGN BY ROBERT BULL

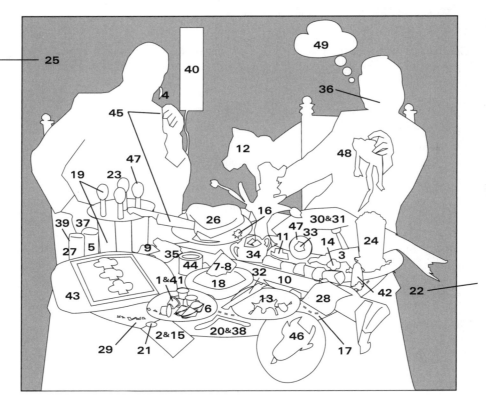

FOR ENUMERATION SEE THE TABLE OF CONTENTS

VILLARD BOOKS NEW YORK / 1992

All rights reserved under International and Pan-American Copyright Conventions. Published in the United States by Villard Books, a division of Random House, Inc., New York, and simultaneously in Canada by Random House of Canada, Limited, Toronto.

Villard Books is a registered trademark of Random House, Inc.

Grateful acknowledgment is made to *New York* magazine for permission to reprint "Penn's Disappearing Cockroach Trick." Copyright © K-III Magazine Corporation. All rights reserved. Reprinted with the permission of *New York* magazine.

Library of Congress Cataloging-in-Publication Data

Jillette, Penn
    [How to play with your food]
    Penn & Teller's how to play with your food/by Penn Jillette & Teller.—1st ed.
      p.   cm.
    ISBN 0–679–74311–1
     1. Humor—Food. 2. Table etiquette—humor.
   I. Teller. II. Title. III. Title: Penn & Teller's how to play with your food. IV. Title:
How to play with your food.
    PN6371.5 P45   1992
    818' .5402—dc20   92–50150

Designed and produced by Robert Bull Design.

Manufactured in the United States of America on acid-free paper.

9 8 7 6 5 4 3 2

First Edition

TO MAKE A CALF'S HEAD BELLOW AS IF ALIVE, WHEN DRESSED AND SERVED UP.

THIS IS EFFECTED BY A SIMPLE AND INNOCENT STRATEGEM; it consists in what follows: take a frog that is alive, and put it at the farther end of the calf's head, under the tongue, which you let fall over it; taking care not to put the frog there till the calf's head is going to be served up. The heat of the tongue will make the frog croak; which sound, coming from the hollow part of the head will imitate the bellowing of a calf as if it were alive.

—*Pinetti's Gift, 1795*

CONTENTS

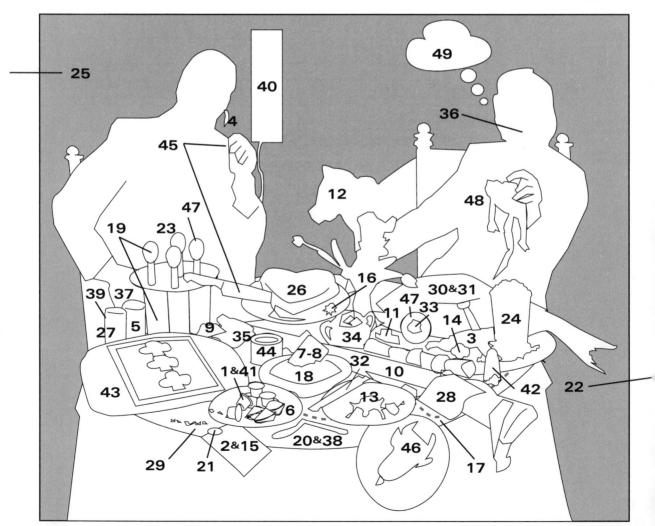

INTRODUCTION [1,2,3]

When your parents or legal guardians said, "Don't play with your food," what they *meant* was "Don't play with your food—unless you can do it *well*." The adults were quickly bored with you squeezing food through your hands and throwing it at them. Anybody would be. It gets old fast. The handling and throwing of food must be used sparingly, as accents. From this book you can develop a good-size repertoire of food tricks. You'll get a chance to throw and handle food, but it'll be in context. It'll be entertaining. Soon, people will be *begging* you to play with your food.

There are plenty of opportunities to use these tricks. Nearly everyone eats, and those who don't eat don't want to see tricks anyway. People who don't eat are too busy trying to find something to eat or working on some political cause. They're really no fun.

You may find this book useful for a few laughs at the tricks, stories, and ramblings. You'll probably enjoy seeing how we did the "Watch Trick" on Letterman (page 118). There are a lot of tricks in this book, and if we inspire you to make a couple of the tricks part of your life, we're honored. Why not make a commitment right now to say "I know" when anyone points out a piece of spinach between your teeth. It's sure not going to do any harm to your social standing or career and it'll make you a better person.

You might want to perfect a couple of tricks to make dining a little more interesting and to get a little more attention. You might enjoy shaking things up, just a touch. Have friends and acquaintances experience tiny miracles in the real world. It doesn't matter that the minor miracles are fake—all miracles are fake. If they weren't fake, they wouldn't be miracles—they would be natural occurrences.

Be careful. If you learn too many tricks in this book and do them all the time you *will* be considered a nut. You will be seen as doing

---

[1] If introductions bore you—cut to the chase and learn a trick. Turn to page 3 right now. It's a trick you can do at the very next meal. You can read this intro later.

[2] If you want to play with the little package of goodies right away, turn to pages 134, 66, 155, and 20 and find out what the hell is in there and how to use it. You can read this intro later.

[3] If you bought this book because we promised you free meals, learn the trick on page 58. Think about it, understand it, practice it. If you get it down, your check will be picked up every time. There are other tricks in the book that could get you free victuals, but this one's the best. You gave us money and we give you a scam that'll put free food in your mouth. That's the deal. You won't ever have to read this introduction. You'll have your money's worth.

tricks not to *enhance* your personality but *instead* of a personality. You will become a Parrot Guy.[4]

Parrot Guy: In the Caribbean (Penn went there before he realized that the best places for vacations were Vegas and R Donuts) there's this Parrot Guy. This is a guy that always shows up at the local tourist hangout with a parrot on his shoulder. He IS the Parrot Guy. And all the vacationers are eager to see him. You go to this certain club at night and there he is, the Parrot Guy. The parrot talks, then people buy the Parrot Guy drinks. This guy uses a bird, living its life (and relieving itself) on his back, in place of a personality. He dresses like a Parrot Guy. He talks like a Parrot Guy. No one talks to him about politics or music or sex or books or art or science or TV or business or movies. He's the Parrot Guy, people talk to him about Parrot Guy things. At this point in his life it would be hard to be anything but the Parrot Guy. If he showed up one day without the parrot, his life would still center around the goddamn bird—"Hey, Parrot Guy, where's the parrot?"

If it appeals to you to become a Parrot Guy, please do so; the world can always use a few more. If you learn and do every trick in this book, you'll be well on your way to Parrot Guydom. There really won't be much time for anything else. There are lots of Parrot Guys in magic, and they can get on people's nerves. Parrot Guys in magic spend their evenings rubber cementing dollar bills together, end to end, so when they need to pay for something, they can roll out the appropriate amount and cut it off with the scissors that they always carry (if this seems like a cool thing to really do—you're definitely a latent Parrot Guy). We respect these people but we can't stand to be around them.

If we all tried to be a little more interesting, tried to say what we really felt, tried to tell the truth as we saw it every once in a while, and used our lying for the entertainment of making wacky things happen,

At right, "Penn" and Teller & Penn and "Teller"

---

[4] Let's talk about the word "guy"—by "guy" we do not mean to leave out women and girls. "Guy" may not please everyone but "guy or gal" would really be odious. In showbiz, "Ladies and Gentlemen" (which also has its problems) has been replaced by "How you guys doing tonight?" as an opener. "How you guys doing tonight?" sucks, but it does show that "guys" is becoming a neutral gender word. That's a good trend and we'd like to extend that to the singular, at least for this intro. There is no shortage of female Parrot Guys.

we might not need Parrot Guys. But thank goodness we have them to talk about, even if we wouldn't want to be snowed in overnight with them at the Twin Cities airport.

If you feel this book is your first step to that long drop off the cliff of becoming a Parrot Guy, we salute you. To the rest of you, have a few laughs, do a few food tricks—but if someone says, "Here comes the Food Guy," make sure that's what you really want.

Thank you for buying our book,

PENN JILLETTE AND TELLER
Parrot Guys

PENN & TELLER'S
HOW TO PLAY WITH YOUR FOOD

STABBING A FORK INTO YOUR EYE

Now that's a title, huh? And the trick is even better. It's a perfect trick. You don't need to bribe anyone. You don't need to set up anything. You don't need to go to a particular restaurant. You don't need to carry any props with you. You don't need to plan (bribing, props, and planning will be covered later in the book). You don't even need to practice! Just read the directions and do it. Hell, just look at the pictures and do it. The more you do it, the better you'll get, but, even the first time out, you'll kill.

The only thing wrong with this trick is that we didn't think of it ourselves. For years we've stared at those "creamers," the little containers that are sometimes cream, sometimes milk, sometimes half-and-half and sometimes, for all we know, white paint. Teller likes to call them "coffee-whiteners." We knew there had to be a trick hidden in those tiny buckets of lightness, we just couldn't get ahold of it. A magician from Kentucky, Mac King, came up with this trick and it's perfect. Mac King[1] is a genius, the Louis Pasteur of diner creeps.

HERE'S ALL YOU DO

Cop a creamer off the table. Maybe "cop" is too jargony—grab, snag, appropriate—just pick up the goddamn creamer when no one is paying attention. (When it comes to creamers, you'll be hard pressed to find a time when anyone *is* paying attention.) When you've got the creamer, hold it in one hand. You don't have to "palm" it. You don't have to grip it in any special way, just hold it upside down in your hand with the tear-away top facing the table. The paper top should be facing away from your thumb—look at the picture. No professional hand position is required but you should be sneaky and keep the creamer out of sight. You don't want anyone wondering why you're fondling a creamer.

Get everyone's attention. In the usual lunch situation, all you have to do is start talking. You can talk about anything. You can even be as direct as "Wanna see a neat trick?"

Pick up your fork with the hand that *doesn't* have the creamer. Bring the fork up near your eye. Tell the people at the table that you've learned this neat trick with your eye. Once you have a fork up near your eye, you'll have everyone's attention. No one wants to miss a nut screwing around with his/her eye and four sharp tines. A fork near the

---

[1] Mac King has his own book coming out called *Tricks with Your Head*. You might want to check it out.

eye, in and of itself, is good entertainment. If you pull down the skin below the eye with the tines of the fork, people really go wacky; it bugs your eye out.

After you've dicked around a little with the fork and your eye, bring up the hand with the creamer as though you were going to look through your fist. Your hand makes a tube around your eye with the plastic bottom of the creamer against your eye. Keep your fingers fairly closed; make sure they don't see the creamer. It's a lot better if the creamer isn't noticed.

Slowly and carefully slide the fork in the outer end of the hand holding the creamer up to your eye.

When the time is right, do these three things at the same time:

1. Puncture the paper top of the creamer with the fork, but be careful—***Don't really stick a fork in your eye!***[2]
2. Squeeze the creamer really hard with the other hand.
3. Scream at the top of your lungs.

Get it? White glop will shoot out of your "eye," all over the table, grossing out and scaring everyone that's watching. It's the best table trick. You can take it from here—you don't need us to tell you which Peter Falk and Sandy Duncan jokes to make.

Mac King is a god.

---

[2] Keep your wits about you. You do have a real honest-to-goodness fork near your real honest-to-goodness eye. Don't get excited and stick the fork through the creamer into your eye. If you have any doubt about how far to stick the fork in to puncture the creamer but not hurt your eye, don't even try the goddamn trick. If you think there's a chance you'll really stick a fork in your eye, forget we even mentioned it.

To do this trick you need to take enough responsibility for your own welfare that you won't stick a goddamn fork in your eye because you misunderstood and thought some book told you to.

If we get a lawsuit against us because we told some idiot to stick a fork ***near*** his or her eye and that cretin sticks a fork ***in*** his or her eye . . . well, it doesn't matter whether it would stand up in court or not, our faith in humanity with its present litigation-happy, it-can't-be-my-fault society will be so shattered that we'll both probably stick forks in each other's eyes just to make the trial more interesting to watch on Court TV.

Believe me, we won't be like Jeffrey Dahmer and just sit there quietly to prove we're crazy.

Be careful.

This trick scares people because it doesn't look like a trick—
it looks like you're a super psychologist with an uncanny knack for
knowing what others want to eat.

HOW TO PREDICT WHAT YOUR FRIENDS
WILL ORDER FOR DINNER

HOW IT APPEARS

You're out to dinner with friends. After they've looked at the menu, but before they announce their choices, you ask them each a few personal questions—about their hobbies, incomes, love lives—anything you're feeling nosy about. You claim their answers contain psychological clues about what your friends feel like eating.

You write down a prediction for each person, fold it up, and isolate it in the middle of the table. Then you call over the waiter/waitress and ask him/her to read out what you have written.

Your "guesses" are all correct. Your friends look at you uneasily, afraid you may know them *too* well.

HOW IT WORKS

We adapted this from a scam "trance channelers" and "psychic readers" use to get information about their clients' dead relatives. It's a little more complicated than poking your eye out with a fork (see page 3). But don't worry; the only special skill it requires is the ability to look your friends straight in the eye and lie (see page 148).

1. The first step of this trick is pure espionage. Before you arrive at the table, you must find out what *one* of your fellow diners is going to order.

   How? Well, you may already know what somebody usually eats. If you were having lunch with Penn, for example, you could count on his ordering turkey on wheat with a lot of mustard and no tomatoes. For Teller it would be Swiss on a bagel with extra tomato. (If the chef forgets and gives Penn the rat-bastard tomatoes, he just passes them to Teller who loves them. That's how enduring partnerships survive.)

   But there are other ways to determine what someone will order. On the way to the restaurant, for example, you could influence somebody's choice by raving about a certain dish. Or when the waiter is naming the daily specials you could see if anyone nods and immediately closes his menu.

   Or you may just want to let your date in on the gag and prearrange for him or her to order a particular dish. Conspiracy is a time-honored way of adding spark to a romance.

2. You arrive at the restaurant, sit down with your friends, and lead the conversation around to the trick. For example, you might say, "Has anybody here read *We Are What We Eat and We Eat What We Do*?" They won't have. It doesn't exist, but it *sounds* like the title of an airport book put out by some anything-for-a-buck publisher like Villard. So they keep listening.

   "It tells how certain activities cause certain food cravings. It sure makes sense that playing tennis and reading *Madame Bovary* leave you hungry for different things."

   It *doesn't* make sense, but they probably won't contradict you. At dinner it's considered rude to say "That is rubbish. Prove it!" even if what the person is saying is transparently silly. Etiquette gives cranks the advantage. So play the role of a crank.

   Continue: "I've gotten really good at guessing what people are going to order. All I have to do is ask you a couple of questions. Want to try it?" They do; they expect you to make a fool of yourself.

   So you go on: "Okay, look over the menu and decide what you want. When you're sure, close the menu and don't tell anyone what you've chosen."

3. Now take out a little pad[1] of paper and hold it so no one can see the page you are writing on. This is important—in fact, the whole trick hinges on it—because you will never be writing what the audience thinks you're writing.

　　Now let's imagine you're doing this trick for your friends, Morty, Carol, Krasher, and Evelyn, and that you've done your espionage-homework (Step 1) on Evelyn and found out she will be ordering Corned Beef and Cabbage.

　　Begin by picking any of the diners *except* Evelyn. Let's start with Morty.

4. MORTY
Ask Morty a few questions about his life (e.g., what time he gets up, how his boss is treating him, whether a cute refrigerator magnet will stick to that screw in his collarbone). It doesn't matter what you ask, as long as you pretend each of his answers is giving you clues about his food preferences.

　　Now nod thoughtfully, and write on your little pad. Everyone *thinks* you are writing down what you think Morty will order for dinner. But they're wrong. Actually, you write:

EVELYN—
CORNED BEEF AND CABBAGE

　　Don't let anyone see what you have written! Fold up the little paper and toss it in the middle of the table (it's more dramatic if you can isolate it in, say, an unused glass or ash tray).

　　Morty thinks you're finished with him. Good. Now pretend you want to check to see how accurate your guess was, like this:

YOU: (*pointing to the folded paper*) Okay, there's my prediction. I won't touch it again. So now you can tell us. What are you going to have?
MORTY: Filet of sole almandine.
YOU: (*nodding as though you got it right*) Potato or rice?
MORTY: Potato—baked—with sour cream and chives.

---

[1]　　Teller likes memo pads. Penn prefers business cards. What matters is that you have as many identical pieces of paper as you have diners.

Voila! Morty has just *told* you what he is going to have for dinner— just what you need to know. Now put that information to use. Pick anyone except Evelyn (you must save her until last). Let's try Carol.

5. CAROL

Ask Carol a few personal questions. Maybe there's some sexy stuff you want to know about her. Go ahead, pry. Remember, it's all for the good of Science.

Act as though you are evaluating Carol's answers and coming to a conclusion, then hold your little pad so no one can see it, and write:

MORTY—
FILET OF SOLE ALMANDINE
BAKED POTATO WITH SOUR CREAM & CHIVES

Tear off the sheet, fold it *exactly the same way you folded the first one* and chuck it in the ash tray or glass with its twin. Now that Carol thinks you have committed your guess to paper, it's time to weasel her choice out of her, like this:

YOU: That's my best guess on you, Carol. You're hard to read. I may have missed it. What did you choose?

CAROL: Steamed vegetables with soy sauce on the side.

...which is exactly what you need to know when you go on to your next victim, Krasher.

6.   KRASHER

Quick! Cover the page to the right of the big black line, and see if you can figure out what you would do when talking to Krasher.

First you	ask your impertinent questions.
Then you	write on your tablet:
	CAROL—
	STEAMED VEGGIES WITH
	SOY SAUCE ON THE SIDE
Then you	fold the paper the same way you did before and put it with the others.
Finally you	"confirm" your prediction by asking Krasher what he's having. He's chosen the Pork Chops.

If you got all these steps right, you're an exceptional pupil. If you claim you guessed "Pork Chops", you're a shameless prevaricator—the ideal character-type for this trick.

7. EVELYN
Ask your phony-baloney, too-personal, psychological questions. Then write:

KRASHER—
PORK CHOPS

Fold the paper just like the others and toss it in.

"Confirm" your "guess", by asking Evelyn what she ordered. You don't actually need to, of course—you *know* all four papers on the table are correct. But asking Evelyn the same way you asked the others throws people off the scent. Surely (they reason) if you *knew* the answer, you wouldn't have to *ask*.

8. Every single little paper has a name and a correct dinner order. The papers look alike. So all you have to do is make sure nobody's keeping track of which paper is whose. That's when you call over the waiter.

Tell him about your strange experiment. Ask him if he'd mind participating. As everybody is listening to his reply, pick up your ashtray or wineglass full of papers and dump them out in front of him. They fall randomly onto the table and the dirty work is done.

All that remains is to sit back and bask in the glory. The waiter reads out each name and order and you are always right.

NOTE: Don't bother predicting what you will order. It's not that impressive to read your own mind.

FINE TOUCHES

1. Don't feel confined to stick to questions about diet and exercise. The big fun in this trick is asking *anything you want*. So go nuts. Ask:

- Physical questions (*Are you allergic to kelp?*)
- Psychoanalytic questions (*If I say "steam shovel," what family member do you think of?*)
- Impudent questions (*How long have you been dyeing your hair?*)

- Intimate questions (*When was the last time you had sex? With whom? Did you enjoy it?*)
- Nosy business questions (*How much did you make last year?*)
- Silly questions (*If you could give a cat to one of the signers of the Constitution, who would it be?*)

2. Take a tip from professional psychics: Make a few minor mistakes. Psychics always do this on the theory that if their answers are too perfect, people will suspect trickery. But if they misspell a name by one letter or draw the "target" design in mirror image, that somehow implies that they got their information by ESP instead of espionage. So now and then get a salad dressing a little off. Or instead of "rare," say "medium rare." Little things like that make it seem more real and give you a nice chance for gags when the waiter is reading out the papers at the end:

   WAITER: ... pork chops, medium rare.
   YOU: (*muttering to yourself*) Dang! I said "rare." I should have known Krasher would have them medium rare from what he was saying about his rubber sheets and baby oil.

3. Spreading pseudoscience and misinformation is not a good thing. So over dessert, confess to your compadres: "Oh, by the way, that thing I did before—guessing your entrees—it wasn't from any self-help book. It was just a trick." They'll ask you how you knew what they were thinking. Say archly, "Oh, I have my sources..." This will leave them *really* worried. If they keep bugging you, recommend this book.

4. If you're dying to do this trick, but haven't been able to find out what Evelyn is going to order, don't worry. Make a *guess*. The trick will still work perfectly for everybody else, but for Evelyn there are two possible outcomes: (a) You luck out and hit it right on the nose. If this happens frequently, forget dining out. Spend that dough at the track. Or (b) You're just wrong. If this happens, blame Evelyn. Gently accuse her of falsifying her "psychological profile" answers for the sake of good taste. She may blush. She may laughingly deny. But if she's gone along with this foolishness so far, you can be sure she's much too well mannered to sneer, "Prove it!"

BUILD A BETTER BANANA

Dreams in their eyes, shampoo in their ears, breakfasters have but a shaky grip on the world. As they try to resurrect consciousness and motor skills, they give off such an innocent, toddlerlike glow that you don't want to do anything too alarming. You just want to give reality a gentle spin.

Imagine Dad shuffling down to the kitchen and serving himself a bowl of cereal. He picks up a banana and peels it, only to find that the fruit inside is *already sliced for him*. For a minute or two, he looks foggily perplexed, trying to remember cutting the banana in his sleep. Then he heaves a sigh and starts to eat.

You're the culprit, of course, but a benevolent sort of culprit. After all, you've stopped Dad from handling a sharp implement in his dangerously uncoordinated condition.

THE SECRET

Get a hat pin long enough to go all the way into the banana and still leave three quarters of an inch sticking out for you to hold on to. Insert the pin into the side of the banana and work it back and forth, slicing all the way through the flesh of the fruit, but leaving the peel intact (except for the pin hole). Pull out the pin and repeat for each slice. By the way, there is another way of accomplishing this, but you don't want to know about it.[1]

Stagger the holes so they're harder to notice. It's best to do this preparation in the morning right before breakfast. If you do it the night before, it allows the banana skin a chance to discolor around the holes and may give you away.

When Dad peels the banana, he may call your attention to the strange phenomenon. Pat him gently on the head, as if pitying someone so confused, and say, "Yeah, sure, Pop. Gene-splicing."

Or, let an uneasy look flicker across your face and murmur, "Wow, I got one like that last week. What do you think it *means*?"

---

[1] Take a needle and thread and pierce the side of the banana between the fruit and the skin. It emerges, say, a sixth of the way around the banana. Reinsert it and repeat the process until you have worked your way around to where you started, forming a loop of thread between the skin and the fruit. Then pull the loop back out through the hole, slicing the flesh. It takes forever to do, and leaves seven pinholes for every slice. See? You didn't really want to know.

A MILKSHAKE AS SELF-DEFENSE

I don't think you'll get a chance to use this trick. I did it only once. Although it's unlikely it literally saved my life, I'm certain it saved me some pain. Consider it a tactical tidbit to keep in the back of your mind. It's like knowing how to get out of a car when it's underwater; chances are you'll never use it but if an applicable situation ever arises you'll be glad you have it in deep storage.

When I graduated from high school in 1973, I believed that little Robert Zimmerman hitchhiked all over the country on his way to becoming Bob Dylan. And I really thought that if I hitchhiked all around the country, Penn Jillette might become a person with a different name that could lead his generation. I went the long way across the country three times, my name is still Penn Jillette, and my generation took its own damn course. If I had spent all those standing-beside-the-road-with-my-thumb-out-and-not-a-thought-in-my-head hours studying math, I might have teamed up with Steve Jobs and changed my generation, but I hitchhiked.

I was eighteen years old and I was on the road. I had very long, wild hair and I wore little wire-rim sunglasses all day and all night. I've never taken a drug or any alcohol in my life but it was my fashion choice to look like the famous junkies I idolized. For 1973 I looked pretty scary (at least as scary as an eighteen-year-old from Greenfield, Massachusetts, can ever look—some people are petrified by dirty down vests). I did my best to look like a rebel.

I was a juggler (I guess I still am a juggler, once you learn you never forget—it's like walking in high heels...er...I mean riding a bicycle). I would do a little street show or juggle as an opener for some awful band in a bar and make a couple–three dollars passing the hat. I really liked that I was living hand to mouth (I didn't count the hundred dollars in traveler's checks from my parents that I had in the lining of my L.L. Bean knapsack). I called my Mom and Dad, collect, every day, but I was on my own. Five dollars from passing the hat would buy me food for a few days while hitchhiking.

For the last few weeks I had been on a vanilla milkshake thing. In *On the Road*, Jack was always eating apple pie with ice cream and I thought if I picked one dessert food and ate only that in different diners all across the country I would keep my name, write a book, and lead the generation directly behind me. I've kept my name, I've cowritten two books, but the generation directly behind me has gone their own damn way, too. I would have been better off sticking to the four major food groups (this was back when meat was a staple, not a condiment).

I got dropped off late at night at a diner in the middle of Nebraska (any place more than three miles from a border, in Nebraska, is the middle). I hadn't eaten all day, I had two or three bucks, and I figured since I was right in front of a diner it was time for my milkshake meal. (Wait a minute! I was only eating milkshakes and I was really thin—I could have invented Slim Fast. Damn! I was closer to changing my generation than I thought.)

I walked in and I was the only customer. Behind the counter was a waitress about my age. I didn't talk to her much, in 1973 I was experimenting with a silent brooding personality (I have since opted for a different personality type). I was clearly on the road and she was clearly in Nebraska, so it's safe to say we were thinking interesting thoughts about each other when I ordered my vanilla milkshake.

In came two guys. I remember them as truck drivers but I remember most people from 1973 as truck drivers. I don't know how old they were (it's impossible to reconstruct the real facts; I've told this story so many times the real facts have disappeared), but they were older than me and they seemed real adult. I would guess late thirties (now that I'm thirty-seven, I always guess late thirties). Common sense would tell me they were smaller than I was (what are the chances of three guys together in a diner in Nebraska in 1973 all being over 6' 6" in a story with no references to basketball or growth hormones?). But they seemed much bigger. They were certainly meaner and much much stronger.

They made some comments about my hair and clothes as they walked by me but I was used to that. That's why I looked like that, so people like those two wouldn't understand me. Everything was fine. I was sitting in my own little world waiting for my vanilla milkshake.

They forgot about me and ordered a couple of cups of coffee. While the waitress was pouring the coffee, they said something to her like "What's a nice girl like you doing in a place like this?"

I lost my mind for a moment. I smiled.

One of the "truck drivers" looked over at me and said, "What are you laughing at, faggot?" (*Nebraska, 1973*)

I pretended not to hear at first and then looked up and said, "I'm sorry, I wasn't listening, I was just lost in my own thoughts."

Then the waitress decided to speak up. She said, "He was laughing at what assholes you guys are." And then she gave me a little flirtatious smile.

I was sunk. But I tried.

"No, no," I said. "I wasn't laughing at all. Certainly not at you."

One of the "truck drivers" then said, "Are you calling this pretty girl a liar?"

Oh-oh—I scrambled. "I definitely wasn't calling her a liar, I just think she misinterpreted my smile. I was just in my own little world, daydreaming."

"You were laughing at us, faggot."

"No I wasn't." I like to think I said that firmly, without gulping or trembling, but if I had to bet, my money would be on gulping and trembling. There may have even been some nausea.

"You calling *me* a liar?" He stood up.

"Oh no. Listen, I'm sorry. I didn't mean any harm. I'm just minding my own business. Please accept my apology for any misunderstanding. I just want my milkshake."

He was walking toward me. At the same time, Little Ms. Death Warrant delivered my milkshake.

"Let's step outside, faggot."

"No sir, if I step outside you're just going to beat me. I don't know how to fight. You'll just beat on me until you get tired. So please leave me alone, I'm really sorry." I said that all rather quickly as he was grabbing my shirt and tugging on it to get me to stand up.

"Well, you're right about one thing, faggot, if you step outside I'm going to beat the shit out of you. But if you stay in here, I'm also going to beat the shit out of you."

He had managed to pull me to my feet. But I yanked away and yelled, "Okay, wait!"

Then, while he backed up and looked at me in surprise, I picked up the vanilla milkshake in its frosty-cold cannister, looked Mr. Truck Driver in the eye, smiled like an idiot, and poured the milkshake over my head. Globs flowed down my hair, over my face and my glasses. It was all over my clothes. It was cold and sticky and no fun.

He was disgusted and disappointed. "This faggot is retarded. He's crazy. I ain't hitting no crazy, retarded faggot."

I kept smiling, but now with reason. I had won. They swore at me some more, pushed me around a little bit, paid for their coffee, and left. I sat there in a tasty frosty puddle. As soon as I saw their truck driving away I began screaming at the waitress. I don't have to go into the exact words—you can make it up as well as I can: I screamed about how she was part of that macho stuff and we were younger and hipper than that and it wasn't funny. I reminded her that I could have gotten really hurt. While I was yelling I was still completely covered with milkshake. I threw down the money for the milkshake and got ready to head to the rest room to try to clean up.

A new character entered. It was the cook, an old guy. I remember him as having "LOVE" and "HATE" tattooed across his knuckles but I think I added that to the story after I heard "Death and Glory" by the Clash.[1] He came out of the kitchen laughing and said he loved the way I handled that situation (notice *he* had handled the situation by hiding in the back room—we were kindred spirits). He took the money I had put down for the milkshake and handed it back to me. He said, "I'm making you a cheeseburger and some french fries. She's going to make you another milkshake and I'm taking the cost of the whole meal out of her pay."

He let me wash up in the big sink in the kitchen. I used industrial Pan-Dandy as a shampoo and wrapped my shirt, covered with dairy products, in wax paper and stuffed it into the bottom of my pack, where I would discover it several days later on its journey to bad cheese.

The cook sat and talked to me while I ate; I don't remember what he said. He probably gave me advice that I could have used to lead someone's generation but I forgot it. The waitress pouted. I had a good meal.

So the self-defense tactic is: **Pour a milkshake over your head.** Even tough "truck drivers" who are full of hate don't want to be sticky.

I remember feeling clever for getting out of an unpleasant situation unharmed. I also remember being sticky for days. Use this technique only in real emergencies.

---

[1]   Yeah, we know it's originally from *Night of the Hunter.* Wanna make something of it?

THE DRIBBLE CAN

SETTING: Informal party where drinks are served in cans.

TARGET: A rival.

OBJECTIVE: The rival has just horned in on a private conversation between you and your date. Your date finds the newcomer too attractive. Attention is turning away from you. You must exterminate the vermin without compromising your *suavité*.

ATTACK: Finish your drink. Wait until you notice your rival's beverage can is almost empty. Then say, "I need another one. May I get you something from the ice chest?"

Relishing the chance to talk behind your back, the conniving charmer will smile and accept: "How thoughtful! I *will* have another."

Go to the bar. Find a "church key"—an ancient pre-pop-top device that punches a triangular hole in the top of a can.[1] Open your drinks, then hook the church key on the top of the rim of your rival's beverage can, and punch a tiny hole in the *side*, three quarters of an inch under the opening he/she will be drinking from.

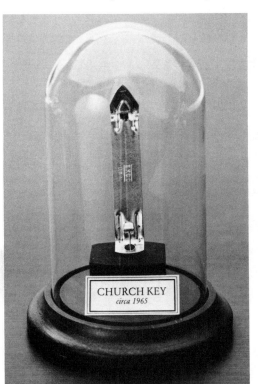

CHURCH KEY
circa 1965

Return, beaming good-naturedly. Hand the sabotaged can to your rival. As he/she starts to drink, liquid will trickle from fingers and chin, creating the illusion of *slobbering*, effectively negating any earlier sex appeal.

The tiny hole is well camouflaged by the printing on the side of a can, but even

For the Purist: *if you use a noncarbonated beverage, like juice or ice tea, then you can puncture the can first and let them pop their own top. With a carbonated beverage you have to pretend to be gracious and open the can for the jerk so that you don't walk across the room with a thin stream of wet gas squirting from your fingers.*

---

[1] It's easier to find nowadays on a Swiss Army knife. Maybe soon we'll find a good use for the fish scaler and magnifying glass.

if the victim thinks of a leak, chances are she/he will hold the can upright while checking—and the dripping will stop! So the cad will be convinced he/she is having a fit of clumsiness.

Distracted, demoralized, *and* disgusting to behold, the soggy seducer shamefully slithers away and the course of true love again runs smooth.

OTHER TARGETS AND USES

1. **In business negotiations:** Offer your opponent a beverage, then watch him try to close a deal while drooling.

2. **At home:** Your spouse is lying on the couch watching TV. He/she waits till you walk by and croons, "Honey, *since you're already up,* would you get me something cold to drink?" Trudge to the fridge[2], doctor the can, and set it on the coffee table. Then return to the kitchen and listen. The delay is the best part. Engrossed in a show, the indolent slob will be subliminally saturated, then suddenly start flapping and swearing. It will make your weekend.

---

[2] **WARNING:** Choose a nonstaining beverage or you'll end up cleaning the upholstery yourself. The lout won't lift a finger.

MAYBE THERE IS SOMETHING TO THIS FORTUNE-COOKIE THING

We never met anyone who believed in fortune cookies. That's astounding. Belief in the precognitive powers of an Asian pastry is really no wackier than belief in ESP, subluxation, or astrology, but you just don't hear anyone preaching Scientific Cookie-ism. The time has come to change that. Working together we can get enough "friend-of-a-friend"[1] stories going to give fortune cookies the credibility every other goofball reality-cheat gets.

If you look in the Gimmicks Envelope, you'll find a bunch of Chinese cookie fortunes. We've spared every expense to get these just right. We used the cheapest paper and ink. We even printed them a little crooked. Except for content, they are indistinguishable from real

---

[1] Jan Harold Brunvand has written lots of cool books about creepy F.O.A.F. urban legends. Check them out.

cookie fortunes. Cut them up. So, when the time comes, all you have to do is:

1. Pick out the correct one, fold it in half, and put it in your pocket the next time you go out with suckers for Chinese.
2. After the meal, when the cookies are delivered, reach into your pocket. Get the P&T fortune and conceal it in your hand.
3. Pick up the cookie with the other hand.
4. Put the cookie on top of our fortune in your hand. Break the cookie with both hands. You now have two fortunes in a hand full of broken cookie. Pick out the P&T fortune, and do your chosen punch line. Don't make this into a magic move—it's just grabbing the correct piece of paper out of crumbs. It's not sleight of hand. No one is looking at you. No one cares; they're all reading their own fortunes.
5. While they're looking at the fortune you switched in, hold the original unfunny fortune with your thumb and dump the cookie crumbs on the table.
6. Wait awhile and then just throw the real one on the floor. You can't screw this up. This move is so easy, Copperfield could do it under the pressure of sorta live TV. It's a day at the beach.

Now, just pick the specific trick you want to do:

To Use

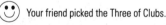
Your friend picked the Three of Clubs.

Sometime during the meal, do the "All-Purpose-Penn-&-Teller-Play-with-Your-Food-Three-of-Clubs-Card-Force" on page 25. (You might want to get them to agree that if you find the right card, they'll pay for your moo shu. That's what we do.)

Try to find the freely chosen card (Three of Clubs) and fail.

Act embarrassed.

Wait until the end of the meal.

When the cookies are delivered, pick up our fortune, read it to yourself, and say, "Did you pick the Three of Clubs?"

When they say "Yeah" you throw our fortune down on the table and let them be amazed.

PENN & TELLER'S

To Use

The chef spit in your food.

Eddie Gorodetsky, the funniest man in the world, thought of this and he's done all the work:

Switch it in.

Say, "I knew I didn't like this place" and throw it down on the table.

To Use

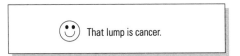

That lump is cancer.

Also from Eddie.

Switch it in.

Say, "Hey, this is kind of depressing," and throw it down on the table.

If you want to go way out there: Earlier in the meal you can casually mention your trip to the doctor and the biopsy that was ordered—but that's really a bit much. It plays very well on its own.

To Use

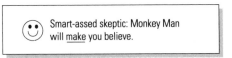

Smart-assed skeptic: Monkey Man will <u>make</u> you believe.

This is a nice creepy trick, that, with a little acting, will give your dining partners serious chills. It's easy to do since all it takes is a lie. It's a long lie called a friend-of-a-friend story. In this case, however, the person telling the F.O.A.F. story (you) knows it's a lie, your basic stupid-skeptic-being-punished-and-converted plot.

During dinner, get on to the subject of the paranormal, or "closed-minded" people, and tell some version of the story below. Don't memorize it. Just read it a couple times to get the main points. It really has to be in your own words, in your own style.

All you have to remember is a skeptical friend-of-a-friend is scared nearly to death and converted after hearing or seeing the prediction "Smart-assed Skeptic—Monkey Man will *make* you believe."

Change the story as much as you want. Make it yours; for the "friend" use a name that a few people at the table know. Ad-lib as much as you want. Just make it good.

Here's the basic story:

This friend of mine called today really upset. He was shook by something that happened to a friend of his. I tried to tell him that there had to be some rational explanation, but my friend wouldn't hear about it. He was totally freaked.

It seems my friend has this other friend at work who was really skeptical. She was really into science and, according to my friend, really closed-minded. She was also into putting people down for any belief they might have in anything. You know the kind.

*So, some guy in this woman-friend-of-a-friend's office was reading the astrology section of the paper aloud at coffee break. He thought it really hit the nail on the head. It was really general, like they always are, but it said something to him about his life. He was getting inspiration from it. When he was done reading, the skeptical woman starts trashing him, making fun of him, and taking away the pleasure this poor guy is getting from his stupid astrology column. Well, the guy is making a pitiful attempt to defend himself. He asks her what sign she is and she says "Pisces" or something, whatever, it doesn't matter. He reads the entry for "Pisces" to everyone in the office. But it's not a regular "There will be a change for the better in your love life" prediction. No, this one reads, "Smart-assed skeptic—Monkey Man will **make** you believe." You can check the paper. My friend said a lot of people had checked the paper for that day and it was in there, under Pisces, "Smart-assed skeptic—Monkey Man will **make** you believe."*

It seemed strange to everyone, but the skeptic just laughed it off. She didn't care, she just went home. The next morning, she didn't show up at work. When her boss called her house, the phone was picked up, but all they heard was loud, apelike grunting. They called a couple of times to make sure they had the right number and kept hearing these horrible nonhuman sounds. Finally, the boss and a girlfriend of hers who had a key went over to the skeptic's house.

*After knocking for a long time they went in and the house was all ripped to pieces and had this strong animal musk smell on everything. On the wall, in lipstick, it said, "Smart-assed skeptic—Monkey Man will **make** you believe." They found the woman, sitting on the floor of her closet. She had all these astrology columns all around her. She was nude and making these ape sounds. But, get this, her hair was white. It was snow white, all the color was gone, and not just the hair on her head, all her hair on her body. All of it.*

My friend says the white-haired woman wouldn't talk about it, she just quit work, and now she's like a fortune-teller or something—professionally, full-time. It was kind of a creepy story. I mean, I guess it was just a really bad dream that she had, and she freaked out and wrecked her own apartment, writing on the walls and stuff. But can your hair lose all its color overnight? If you're almost scared to death, can your hair lose all its pigmentation?

If your friends don't greet your story with much skepticism, you should get new friends. When they start attacking and laughing at the story and poking holes in it, join in. Say it seems pretty farfetched. All the while you're trashing the story, keep insisting that it's weird because the friend that told you this story never lies.

Let it get really cruel. Make fun of your friend and talk about what a load of garbage all predictions are. Try to time this so that you're really trashing the whole idea of the paranormal when the fortune cookies come.

Don't mention that fortune cookies are predictions.

Take a cookie and switch in our fortune.

Let everyone else read their fortunes out loud but you just sit there silently. Let them all keep laughing but you freeze up and let your face go blank. Trembling a little is a nice touch.

Don't ever read the "Monkey Man" fortune aloud, just keep staring at it. Eventually someone will take it out of your hand and read it to the others.

It's a cute little *Twilight Zone* moment.

Maybe you can convince the most attractive person at the table to spend the night with you to keep you safe.

If you want to go all the way, trash your apartment, write on your walls, and bleach your hair. All your hair. Who knows, you might look good platinum. You're sure as hell going to make more money as a fortune-teller.

THE ALL-PURPOSE-PENN-&-TELLER-
PLAY-WITH-YOUR-FOOD
THREE-OF-CLUBS CARD FORCE

To read this chapter, get a pack of cards and go to your room.

Uh-oh, you think. *This sounds like work.* Yup. But we're asking you to invest half an hour in learning something that will make you a god to your friends for the rest of your life. It's going to be worth it.

A magic trick, like a joke, has two parts: a Setup and a Payoff. In a Setup, something unamazing happens (for example, you take a card, memorize it, and shuffle it back into the deck). Then, in the Payoff, something impossible occurs (the card appears under the pot roast). What the audience doesn't know is that during the Setup, you have done the sneaky stuff that makes the amazing Payoff possible.

So we're going to teach you a Setup. Note we say *a.* Singular. You need only one. Why? Because your friends never remember the Setup; all they care about is the Payoff. They don't get excited about shuffling; they want to see the Three of Clubs appear in their squab. If you do the same Setup with fifteen different Payoffs, your friends think they've seen fifteen different tricks. So although learning a good Setup is work, you'll reap the rewards again and again.

But what type of setup should you learn? There are basically two methods of take-a-card tricks:

1. Your friend freely selects a card, then you go through godawful fancy gyrations (not that we're trying to prejudice you) to locate it. These moves are tricky—if your finger slips, you can easily lose control of the card and get all the way to the Payoff with the *wrong one.* Imagine diving into your friend's bowl of pasta, pulling out a marinara-soaked pasteboard, and asking with glee, "Is this your card?" only to have your friend reply disgustedly, "No."

2. You make your friend pick the exact card you need for the Payoff. Such a maneuver is called a *force.* If you *force* a particular card at the beginning, all the work is done before your friend even realizes you've started the trick. This method also lets you prearrange spectacular Payoffs, like having a pizza delivered with your force card spelled out in pepperoni (see page 165). We think a force is the superior choice. It's sure-fire and lets you concentrate on dramatizing the Payoff instead of fretting about juggling the cards. Now, some magic-hobbyists who love learning zillions of precise little

moves (these characters are known in the biz as "finger-flingers") would tell you this is the lazy way out. Such people should remember that the wheel got invented only because some fourth- or fifth-millenium B.C. Mesopotamian was too lazy to lug bricks.

We're going to offer you four versions of this force, so you can pick the one that suits your personality type.

VERSION 1: A Superb Force for People Who Want to Learn Some Genuine Professional-Quality Sleight-of-Hand[1]

In your typical performing situation, you will be borrowing a pack of cards. Your first step is to get the force card, the Three of Clubs, to the face of the pack.

1. Spread the cards toward yourself and locate the Three of Clubs. If anybody notices you looking at the cards, say, "I need to remove the joker, or the trick won't work." This is what is technically termed "Misdirection," which means "lying to make the trick work."

   As soon as you spot the Three of Clubs, cut it to the bottom of the pack. Continue to spread the cards until you find the joker. Remove it and toss it aside.

CUT HERE

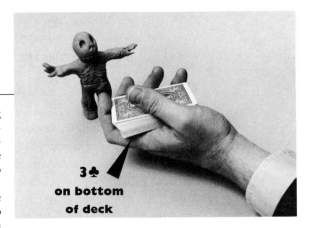

2. Place the pack of cards face down on your left[2] hand, with your index finger curled up at the outer end.

3♣ on bottom of deck

---

[1] If you just can't stand the idea of handling playing cards, we can understand your feelings. Skip this section and follow the directions on page 31 for "VERSION 2: An Only Slightly Inferior Force for People Who Hate Using Their Hands But Are Willing to Remember a Little Arithmetic."

[2] It doesn't really matter which hand. If you're more comfortable using the other hand, feel free to go through this whole set of directions and write in "right" where we have "left," and "left" where we have "right." It's your book now, and you're entitled to make it as personal as you want.

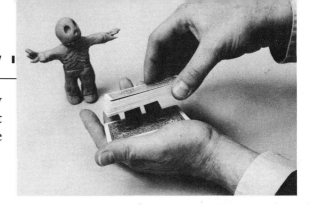

uffle: Start by
your right
lift off three

4. P .... inward,
   bu .... tips of
   the

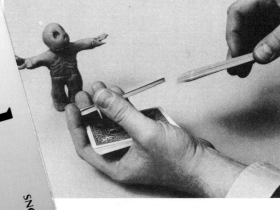

5. Pull the pac

6. ...and allow the cards
   tips to drop on to th
   rest.

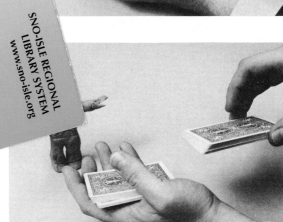

April

National Poetry Month

Year of the BOOK

7. Repeat. That is, bring the right-hand packet over the left hand again. Allow the left thumb and forefinger to retain a few more cards, and draw them off as the right hand pulls its packet clear.

Then once again drop the cards from the left fingertips on to the palm.

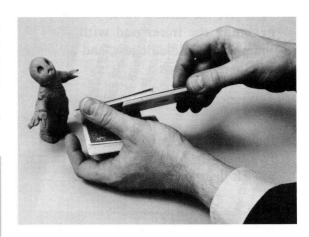

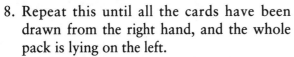

TIP: This whole process is easier and more secure if you tilt the outer end of the pack in the left hand slightly downward.

8. Repeat this until all the cards have been drawn from the right hand, and the whole pack is lying on the left.

Congratulations. You have just completed your first False Shuffle.

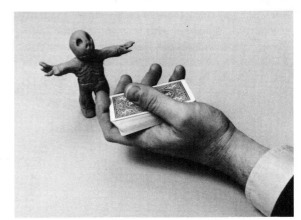

9. If you have done this correctly, the Three of Clubs will still be at the bottom or face of the pack.

10. Now *force* the card: Turn to your friend and say, "This time as I shuffle, I want you to say, 'Stop!' whenever the urge comes upon you." You begin the shuffle again, but with one difference: *This time you start by lifting the entire deck off your left palm.*

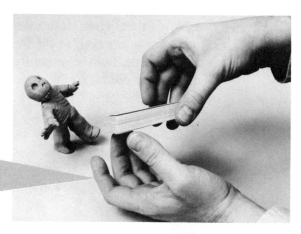

NOTE: No cards left here.

11. Repeat the movements of the shuffle (the left fingers skim off and retain little packets of cards as the right hand pulls its packet out of the way). Continue until you hear "Stop!"

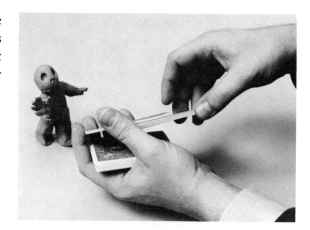

12. Then freeze. Say, "Remember the card you stopped me at!" and *immediately show your friend the bottom card of the packet in your right hand.* As you do so, add "I won't peek," and turn your head away.

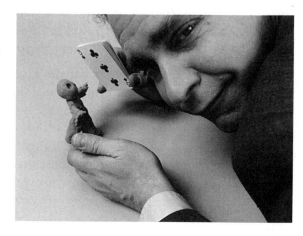

Now in reality all you are doing is showing your friend the Three of Clubs that has been at the bottom of the right-hand packet throughout the shuffle. But the unfamiliar style of shuffling and your matter-of-fact attitude confuse your friend into imagining that saying "Stop!" determined the card.

> **TIP:** Be sure to say, "I won't peek," and turn your head when showing the card. Psychologically, it seems to rule out the possibility that you already know what the card is by suggesting that you would like to peek at the card, but are too ethical to do so. Yeah, right.
>
> **ANOTHER TIP:** Be forceful in asking your audience to remember the card. If there are several people at the table, make sure they all see it. You don't want to come to the climax of your trick, say triumphantly, "Is this your card?" and hear the wavering reply, "I guess...could be..."

13. When your audience has engraved the card in its memory, slap the cards in your right hand onto the cards in your left hand, square the deck, and hand it to the person who "selected" the card, saying, "Give those a good shuffle, will you?"

That's it. The unamazing part is all done. Now turn to page 35 and learn how you can wow them in a fancy restaurant. Page 165 tells you how to get a pizza delivered that features the punch line. Going out for Chinese? Look on page 20.

And after you get the hang of it, start making up your own punch lines. Ice a birthday cake with three big clubs[3] and the motto

"IS THIS YOUR CARD?"

and have Sister flip off the lights and Dad march in with the lighted cake while Mom concentrates on her card.

But don't stop with food. If you're a scuba diver, arrange your message in shells on the ocean floor and deliver the punch line at fifty feet. If you're a stripper, get a tattoo of the Three of Clubs in a really good place, and reveal it as the climax of your act. If you're a millionaire, hire a skywriter and wait for your guests to look up.

---

[3] Someday you may realize you don't *have* to use the Three of Clubs.

VERSION 2: An Only Slightly Inferior Force for People Who Hate Using Their Hands But Are Willing to Remember a Little Arithmetic[4]

1. Have somebody else shuffle the pack. You don't want to touch it any more than you absolutely have to.

2. Take back the pack and spread it. Locate the Three of Clubs and cut it to a position tenth from the top of the pack. Just spot the three as you spread the cards, then count nine cards on top of it, and cut the pack. Use the cover story about needing to eliminate the jokers (see step #1 of the hands-on force above).

3. Hand the pack to your friend (feels good to get rid of it, eh?). Tell your friend to name a number between ten and twenty (for example, sixteen) and deal that number of cards onto the table.[5] Now instruct your friend to put down the pack and pick up the packet just dealt.

4. Say, "To randomize the choice a bit more, let's add the two digits of your number, one and six. That makes seven. Deal seven cards onto the table." When the instructions have been carried out, point to the back of the seventh card (which of course works out to be the Three of Clubs) and say, "Look at that card and memorize it. I won't peek." Turn your head away. (See TIP and ANOTHER TIP on page 30.)

5. Then have the deck shuffled and you're ready to knock 'em dead.

---

[4] If even this is too much effort, skip to page 32 and the force labeled, "VERSION 3: A Good Force for Slugs Too Lazy to Manipulate Cards or Remember Simple Arithmetic, But Who Have a Knack for Brazen Bluffing."

[5] If they pick ten, that's fine. If they pick twenty (they won't), say, "I said *between* ten and twenty," and make them pick again. Ixnay entytway.

VERSION 3: A Good Force for Slugs Too Lazy
to Manipulate Cards or Remember Simple Arithmetic,
But Who Have a Knack for Brazen Bluffing[6]

1. Have the pack shuffled. Then get the Three of Clubs to the top (or back) of the deck. Use the same basic procedure described in step #1 on page 26. On second thought, if you've selected this force, then you might find the effort of turning book pages a wee taxing. So here, reproduced for your convenience, is what it says on page 26:

> Spread the cards toward yourself and locate the Three of Clubs. If anybody notices you looking at the cards, say, "I need to remove the joker, or the trick won't work." This is what is technically termed "Misdirection," which means "lying to make the trick work."

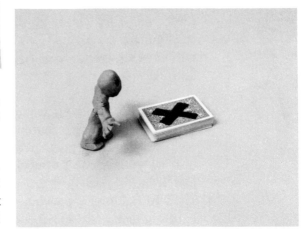

As soon as you spot the Three of Clubs, cut it to the top of the pack. Place the cards on the table.

*The card with the big, stupid **X** is the Three of Clubs. The **X** is there just to make the directions clear. Do **not** draw a big, stupid **X** on the back of your force card.*

2. Say to your friend, "Cut off around half the pack and put your packet here." Point to a spot nearby on the table. Your friend cuts.

Your friend cuts the cards.

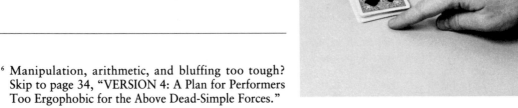

---

[6] Manipulation, arithmetic, and bluffing too tough? Skip to page 34, "VERSION 4: A Plan for Performers Too Ergophobic for the Above Dead-Simple Forces."

3. Say "Good." Pick up the half of the pack your friend left behind and put it crosswise on the half he's just set down, and say, "Let's mark where you cut."

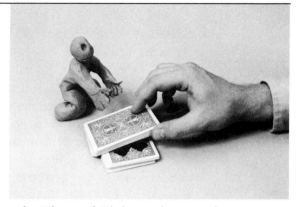

Put the remainder of the deck crosswise on the packet your friend cut off.

4. See what you've done? You've put the Three of Clubs at the top of the lower half of the deck, just below the cut. But if you were to ask your friend to take that card right now, he/she might remember which half is which and catch your scam. So you take a moment to help your friend forget. Momentarily take the attention off the cards. Choose a distraction that suits your style:

Romantic: Look at your companion and exclaim, "Wow, you look spectacular tonight! You're such a knockout! You're making it really hard to concentrate." Touch knees under the table.

Sporting: Say, "Card tricks are dull if there isn't a little something riding on them." Reach into your pocket or purse and bring out a hundred-dollar bill. Drop it on the table. Add, "If I finish this meal without finding your card, Mr. Franklin goes home with you." Avarice is mighty misdirection.

Crude: Blow your nose. Have an attack of choking. Look across the room or out the window and say, "Is that somebody famous?" Tell a joke. Stick a fork in your eye (see page 3).

Take the attention off the cards for a moment.

5. Now that the spectator has lost track of which half is which, point to the back of the Three of Clubs, and say, "Pull out the card you cut to and remember it. I won't look." Turn your back. If others are present, tell the person who selected the card to show it around to everybody.

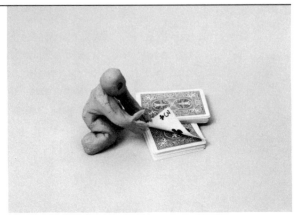

6. Tell the spectator to return it to the pack and shuffle the cards. Then go into your big Payoff.

VERSION 4: A Plan for Performers Too Ergophobic[7] for the Above Dead-Simple Forces

1. Go into partnership with someone smaller and less talkative than yourself.
2. Have him do the Force for you while you talk. Tell him it's division of labor and assure him that talking is the hard part.

---

[7] Work-shy. Now use it three times and it's yours.

THE JAMES BOND FANCY-SCHMANCY
RESTAURANT CARD TRICK

Here's a thought experiment: Picture Bruce Springsteen. Got him? Replace his guitar with a deck of cards. Okay? Give him as much skill with sleight of hand as he has with a guitar (i.e., barred E Major chord = competent card force). Got the image? Will Bruce Springsteen, E Street Shuffler, get laid? Well, maybe—he's still from Jersey. But you'll have to agree that his sexual equity takes a pretty big dip when rocking changes to conjuring.

It's not very mysterious. Music is sexier than magic. Elvis (the dead one) in *Jailhouse Rock*, didn't make eye contact with the ingenue, curl his lip, and say "Freely choose a card, any card, from this perfectly ordinary deck, baby." He rocked. The way you move, rocking with a guitar, looks like sex. The way you move, false-shuffling a deck of cards, looks like knitting.

All is not lost, though. There's always James Bond. James Bond never did a card trick, but you can picture James Bond (let's all picture preponytail Connery) doing a card trick and looking cool. Bond handled cards in whatever the Vegas Bond movie was and Ian had him ring in a cooler[1] in one of the books. It's not a far reach to see him flourishing Ms. Galore's randomly selected card across a dinner table. It's still a bit of a stretch but it's not out of the question.

Whenever we go to a fancy-schmancy restaurant, we feel like James Bond. There must be a female equivalent of James Bond for women to look up to, but we can't think of her. (Maybe there isn't a female James Bond role model. Maybe that's part of what the Women's Movement is all about. Hmmm.) In a fancy-schmancy restaurant, feeling like James Bond (or what's-her-name), you couldn't pull out a dirty dog-eared deck and say, "Hey, you guys wanna see a card trick?" But you could mention that you'd seen an amusing little card maneuver in Monte Carlo that you would like to show them. You could politely call the server over and slip him or her a twenty to run out and buy you a deck of cards.

If you could then, with no effort, sneak the chosen card out of the deck and into an entree—that might be okay cool. It's not "Louie Louie," but it's a killer card trick. It's as cool as a card trick is ever

---

[1] To "ring in a cooler" is cardsharper slang meaning to switch the deck in use for a stacked one. If Ian Fleming had known this phrase, he would have used it.

going to get, and we've got it all set up for you[2] in sixteen of the finest restaurants in the world. Remember this trick the next time you're in one of the neighborhoods listed below.

We've gone to the managers of all these restaurants. We've given them all decks of cards and zillions of duplicate Threes of Clubs (goddamn, we love that card). We've run the restaurant employees over their part of the trick. They're all restaurants that we really like, really fancy-schmancy restaurants with great food, and they're all ready to do their part of making this trick happen for you.

---

[2] Man, oh, man, we're trying like hell to have this all set up for you. We're working like crazy monkeys to get these restaurants ready. Bruce Springsteen is a superstar and all he can do is get thirty-five thousand people to raise their arms in the air, wave them back and forth, and occasionally count to four in unison. We're substars and we're trying to get restaurants around the world to stock decks of cards and slip extra Threes of Clubs into food. It's a lot harder.

Lots of things could screw us. Some of these restaurants may change management. This book may bomb and everyone may forget that they promised us they'd keep this trick going. This book may be too successful (we're really sweating this one) and the restaurants may run out of cards right when you want to do the trick. A breed of non-indigenous evil restaurant vermin that eats only playing cards that have been exposed to grease-steamy kitchen air could be released as part of an evil plot by Harry Blackstone, Jr., to bring us finally to our wretched knees. Maybe you're reading this book 273 years from now, after finding it in a landfill that you're excavating to see how we lived back then (I guess all the videotape was destroyed or maybe you can't figure how to set the clock on the VCR), but the trick sounds cool to you, and all restaurants and even the idea of "restaurant" were destroyed in the big Mad-Max-Terminator-H.-G.-Wells-plot-device war, and you still want to do the trick.

Or maybe there's something's wrong on your end. Maybe you live in one of the many godforsaken but still delightful places that aren't listed below. Maybe you don't even visit these cities. Maybe the fine (but ever-so-slightly-overpriced) restaurants we chose aren't to your taste. Maybe you don't want to spend your hard-earned bread on fancy restaurants. Maybe you're saving up to see P&T live when we bring our breathtaking extravaganza to your town, city, or godforsaken rural route. Maybe you have a restaurant you love and go to all the time and would prefer to do the trick there.

Maybe we're lying and never lifted a finger to make this trick really work.

So, better safe than sorry. Even if the restaurant is listed below, give a call and make sure they're all set up (if they aren't, call Villard—not us). If the restaurant you want to go to isn't listed below, it's not hard to set it up yourself. Explain the trick, give them a deck, an extra Three of Clubs, and a good tip.

We really hope it all goes as planned and all the preproduction is done for you. We're trying. If you do have to set it up yourself, look on the bright side: If you set it up yourself, you can use any card you want—you aren't stuck with the goddamn Three of Clubs.

Here's all you have to do:

Learn the "All-Purpose-Penn-&-Teller-Play-With-Your-Food Three-of-Clubs Card Force" on page 25. Learn it really well—the meal is going to cost you a couple-two-three dollars. You don't want to be the one to drop the ball.

Make reservations in any one of the restaurants listed below. While you have them on the phone make sure they're all set up to do the Penn & Teller Three of Clubs trick.

When you get to the restaurant say your name like this: last name—pause—first name, last name. For example "Bond—James Bond," "Steinem—Gloria Steinem," "Jillette—Penn Jillette," or "Teller—Teller."

Tell your date or your party that you saw an amusing little card maneuver in Rio; be dignified and understated (remember, you're Bond or that female equivalent, whose name is on the tip of our tongue). Call the server over and ask to **have the maître d'** send out for a deck of cards. The "maître d'" part is really important. You may be waited on by a new employee, and you want the maître d' to have a chance to explain the trick.

Give the server a twenty for the cards. (We've already given them the cards free; the twenty is a tip for the extra work the server is going to do. He/she deserves it.) The server will bring you the cards and make a note of which person at your table is picking the card. When that person orders an entree, the server will put a note next to it and the cook will put one of zillions of threes of clubs we've given them right into the victim's food. If it's broiled fish—they'll slide it under the fish. If it's pasta—they'll slip it in the bowl. You get the idea. The restaurant will do it right. These are classy places.

Meanwhile, back at the table: You open the fresh deck of cards, fan them out in front of you, and show disapproval. Rub your fingers over the deck and make a cryptic, snooty but still cool comment like, "Deplorable! A restaurant of this caliber should be able to find a deck of cards with an English silk finish. I hope I can work with these."

Set up the "All-Purpose-Penn-&-Teller-Play-With-Your-Food Three-of-Clubs Card Force" (on page 25) in plain view. All magicians do stuff like this in plain sight all the time and never get caught. Bond (or Double-0-What's-Her-Face) will have no trouble at all. Remember: Stay cool, no nerd moves tonight. You have a license to kill.

Shuffle the selected card (our friend, the Three of Clubs) back into the deck. Let someone else cut. It has nothing to do with the trick but

James (or Jane, maybe we should just go with Jane Bond. Nah, that's much too cheesy) would have someone else cut.

Pick up the deck, pull out a random card (check and make sure it's not the Three of Clubs, you don't want to get lucky and blow the trick). Say "Is this your card?"

It isn't.

Don't be flustered, you work for Her Majesty's Secret Service, it can't be your fault. It must have been that inferior American linen finish.

Shrug. (You're cool enough without some stupid trick.) Just stick the cards in your pocket or purse (you don't want people snooping through the deck later).[3]

Wait until they get their entree and, **get this!**—you now reach into their hot, tasty, expensive food and pull out the Three of Clubs that the cook snuck in and say, "Is this your card?"

Granted, it's hard to picture Mr. or Ms. Bond reaching into someone else's food but, trust us, it's amazingly cool.

No one will guess that you set it up with the cook (*you* didn't, *we* did) they'll just think you're the coolest sleight-of-hand wizard secret agent they've ever seen.

It ain't quite rock 'n' roll, but you'll like it.

---

[3] If you want to gild the lily and cover your ass five ways from Friday, you can do a slightly fancier version: After the card has been returned and cut into the pack, spread the cards in a fan so that you can spot the Three of Clubs. Cut the pack above the Three so that it ends up on top. Now present the bottom card (a random one) as if you think it's the selected card. When it's not, do the reaction described, and put the cards in your pocket or purse with the Three against your body. That way, if, after the revelation, some intelligent pest should say, "Aw, it's not the same Three of Clubs!" you can reach into your pocket/purse, *push off the original Three of Clubs and leave it in your pocket* while you bring out the rest of the cards and toss them smirkingly onto the table. Smile and say with a thinly-disguised sneer of condescension, "Rather a naive suggestion. But here, search the deck for duplicates. I find skeptics amusing."

SIXTEEN COOLEST FANCY RESTAURANTS IN THE WORLD

Campanile
624 South La Brea
Los Angeles, CA 90036
213-938-1447

BIX
56 Gold St.
San Francisco, CA 94133
415-433-6300

The Blue Room
1 Kendall Square
Cambridge, MA 02142
617-494-9034 (Ask for Chris or Stan)

Palace Cafe
605 Canal St.
New Orleans, LA 70130
504-523-1661

Belgo (same-day reservations only)
72 Chalk Farm Road
London, England NW1 8AN
(0) 71 267 0718

Hat Dance
325 W. Huron St.
Chicago, IL 60610
312-649-0066

Mark's Place
2286 N.E. 123rd St.
North Miami, FL 33181
305-893-6888

Auberge du Pommier
4150 Yonge Street
Toronto, Ontario M2P 2B5
416-222-2220

Le Square Trousseau
1 Rue Antoine Vollan
Paris 12 France
33143430600

The Cajun House, La Maison Cajun
1219 Mackay
Montreal, Quebec H3G 2H5
514-871-3898

Kables at The Regent
199 George Street
Sydney, 2000 Australia
61-2-238-0000, ask for Kables reservations

Famous Bill's
30 Federal St.
Greenfield, MA 01301
413-773-9230

THE PARSLEY GAME

We've spent a lot of time on the road together. A lot of time. We mean, lots of time. We're talking, coming up on twenty years here—a long, long time. Before laptops, all we had was a tape deck full of Lou Reed, Residents, Jonathan Richman, NRBQ (and, if truth be told, some less hip stuff), as well as conversation with each other and whatever co-workers were along, to keep us from jumping ship and getting a job at a Highway 61 Stuckey's. If late-night talk shows lean any more toward private jokes and "Twenty Questions"[1] skills, we may be prepared to host.

During the welcome restaurant stops, we invented the "Parsley Game." It's a game that honed our professional skills and tested the human qualities we most admire: deceit, misdirection, subterfuge, vigilance, guile, aggression, and bribery. You might enjoy playing it.

The Parsley Game is very simple: When parsley, that useless biennial bastard nephew of the carrot family, is served on your plate as a garnish, you sneak it onto the plate of one of your dining partners, without being seen by the recipient. It's as easy as that, but, like chess, the possibilities are endless, and long after the World Chess Grandmaster is a computer, we'll still have a human Parsley champ (but, of course, she'll be fifteen years old and Eastern European). The first few times you play the game, you'll win, but then your pals will catch on that you're playing and it will get harder.

A FEW TIPS

When your entree is delivered, quietly get your parsley into your hand and get that hand into your lap so your parsley is forgotten. Soon everyone you know will be doing the same thing. It's nice and it keeps everyone's elbows off the table. Parsley accomplishes what a thousand years of Mom-yelling couldn't.

---

[1] This doesn't tie in with food, but a great way to play Twenty Questions is to wait until you're "it" and play with nothing particular in mind. You pick "animal," "vegetable," or "mineral" at random and from there on just answer "yes" or "no" by whim.

If you don't want to get caught, say "yes" to the first guess after question number fifteen that fits all the previous answers.

Use care. If other players start saying stuff like, "Let me see . . . what's 'animal', red, bigger than a 1983 Honda, diaphanous, and only found in New Jersey?" you're sunk.

One of us is no longer allowed to play Twenty Questions.

Ever!

Distractions will work for the first six or seven games. Believe it or not, pointing over the victim's shoulder and saying, "Is that the guy from the bowling alley?" works better than "You wouldn't think Uma Thurman and Mel Gibson would be together, naked, right over there, would you?"

After a while, no one will turn around for anything. The most surreal events in the Parsley Game (and we didn't make this up, we swear on our eyes this happened) came when a bunch of us were out eating Indian food[2] on Sixth Street. There was no parsley garnish on the Indian food but when you've played Parsley for a while, you stay jacked and ready. There were about eight of us; Marc Garland, our original Director of Covert Activities, and Penn had their backs to the front window. A car on the street went out of control and crashed through the front window of the restaurant. It was deafening, everyone screamed. But Marc and Penn didn't even turn around. They went into the Parsley defense position, staring at their plates. Only the front wheels of the car came into the restaurant and no one was hurt, but that didn't matter. If the car burst into flames and J. D. Salinger walked out of the wreckage singing "La Bamba" in Hebrew, Penn and Marc would not have turned around.

When distraction stops working, sleight of hand will come into play. Tracy Gable, a friend who sold our T-shirts for a while, would ask to try something on your plate, reach over with her fork to get a taste, and deposit her parsley from her palm.

Props can help. Noticing Teller's water glass was low, Penn dropped his parsley into the opaque water pitcher and poured himself a glass, gingerly, without letting the parsley pour out. When Teller held his glass out, Penn let the water float the parsley into Teller's glass.

Teller once got sick of dicking around and did it right. He slipped a waiter twenty bucks to serve Teller no parsley and put enough on the other plates to bury the food.

Have fun.

---

[2] You can calm down about the condiments with Indian food. We had dinner with a big Pakistani cheese; he's a honcho mathematician, a prince or something, and some sort of cricket star, a really cool guy from Pakistan (which is close enough to India for us), and he said that you could put any Indian condiments on any Indian food you wanted. It was a big relief. We were always worried that we were doing the Southern Asia equivalent of putting ketchup, cream, and grape jelly on pastrami. (Take this information with a grain of curry, however; he could have been just setting us up to be humiliated when we play "Kanchipuram.")

THE OLIVER STONE MELON-HEAD TRICK

Oliver Stone's movie (he probably calls it a "film") *JFK* came out at the end of 1991 and caused a pretty big ripple in the press. *JFK* is no longer a hot topic but the President of the United States being shot in the head dead is important enough to make our following stunt topical for a good long while.

In Dallas, in 1963, investigators were lucky to have one home movie camera covering the Presidential motorcade during the assassination. If the President were shot at a public event in the 1990s, we would have it from over a hundred angles and in every format: VHS, 8mm, and one old guy with Beta. If John Fitzgerald Kennedy were assassinated today, it's likely Lee Harvey Oswald would have a HI-8 on a tripod in the Texas School Book Depository Building and smile into it before firing. We are living in an age that is very well documented.

It may seem like this has nothing to do with playing with your food but stay with us on this. It's a great bit.

One of the things that's pointed out repeatedly by conspiracy hobbyists is Kennedy's head jerking "back and to the left" when the bullet hits in the Zapruder film. In *JFK*, "back and to the left" is repeated enough that Ollie seems like he's trying to start a dance craze.

Intuition sure sides with the conspiracy argument. It would seem that if the head goes "back and to the left" the bullet would have come from "front and to the right"; the grassy knoll, the overpass, the train yard, LBJ, CIA, FBI, Q.E.D. It's just Newtonian physics, action-reaction stuff, right?

We don't know if there were other gunpersons. You sure aren't going to get us to go on record saying Oswald acted alone. We just don't have enough facts. We weren't even near Dallas on that day and we can prove that much. But we do have a fun trick that raises some questions and will impress the hell out of your friends. It's a lot of work, but it's worth it.

In the September 1976 issue of the *American Journal of Physics* 1968 Nobelist (hydrogen bubble chamber stuff) Luis W. Alvarez of Lawrence Berkeley Laboratory did a little bit of good old experimental physics on the assassination. He explained that a bullet penetrating a skull does not transfer much of its energy to the head. It's a little thing going really fast and it just kind of slides right in. The brain offers little resistance, but when the bullet pops out the other side of the head, it pulls with it lots of the gunk that used to think. This bullet and brain-whiz make a little jet blast that pushes the head in the opposite direc-

tion (the old action-reaction thing). That is to say, it pushes the head *toward* the bullet's point of origin. Wow. People have done experiments. They've shot corpses and animals in the head and the head jerks toward the gun.

Even creeps like us couldn't really include shooting corpses in a food book as "a trick you can do at home," but Luis said that he and a buddy with a deer rifle had done the same experiment with a melon wrapped in one-inch Scotch glass filament tape. Bingo! Now we're talking! A melon is food. And shooting a melon wrapped in fiberglass tape with a 6.5mm Mannlicher-Carcano rifle—if that isn't playing with your food, then I'm a blue-nosed gopher and Jim Morrison *was* a genius.

We shot some fiberglass-wrapped melons and it's amazing.

THE DIRECTION OF THE SHOT

Melon No. 3

Melon No. 16

Melon No. 35

HERE'S ALL YOU DO

1. Get a permit for a gun. The Second Amendment to our Constitution is still there and you can get a permit in every state unless you have a police or dangerous psychological record. (We were shooting in a controlled environment with cops and stuff around so our records didn't need to be checked.)

2. Get ahold of a rifle. We used a 6.5mm Mannlicher-Carcano rifle, the same model that Oswald fired, but we were just showing off. Any high-power rifle will do. After shooting the Mannlicher ourselves, we had Herb, our shooter (that's him to the right), fire lots of different rifles to get the prettiest picture. Every single melon that moved—moved toward the gun.

3. Find a rifle range. You don't want to do this in your backyard, unless you live in a place where they're used to gunfire—like Times Square or Graceland.

4. Get some fiberglass tape. We used one-inch Scotch glass filament tape, the same kind used by Luis W. Alvarez in 1969 at the San Leandro Municipal firing range, but we were just showing off. Any fiberglass tape will work.

5. Get a melon. We used a honeydew, the same kind Oswald had for breakfast on November 22, 1963, but we were just showing off. Any head-sized melon will work.

6. Wrap the tape around the melon. Get it so it's a nice even skull-like thickness.

7. Decorate your fiberglassed melon. Penn drew a picture of Oliver Stone on his. Teller used "Think Globally—Act Locally." We both feel strongly that putting a melon wearing a pink pillbox hat next to the target melon is in very bad taste.

8. Set your melon head on the range. If you want to do it perfectly, have the melon 265 feet from your symbolic book depository (even we didn't do this, and we were showing off).

9. Shoot the melon with the gun (extra credit for getting three shots off in 3.2 seconds).

That's it. We did it and it was awesome. Your friends will be amazed. The melons jump right toward you. Way counterintuitive.

We're not saying anything about who shot Kennedy but after you've shot a few melons, you might want to fire a quick letter off to Mr. Stone and ask him why he didn't try this. The *American Journal of Physics* hasn't been sealed. He'll probably just tell you that Newton was clearly part of the conspiracy.

THE IRISH TEA TRICK

Your friend writes an initial on a sugar cube, then melts it in a cup of tea. After suitable hoodoo, the initial appears *on the palm of your friend's hand.*

This is not an Irish trick, and the tea isn't essential, either—you could just as well use a glass of water. It's a trick with a sugar cube. But brisk tea and bogus tradition enhance the witchy ritual.

PREPARATION

Have handy some sugar cubes, a spoon, and a no. 2 or softer pencil. Then make some tea for your friend (if you go for the Irish presentation, you might as well make it Irish Breakfast).

PRESENTATION

1. Ask your guest, "Do you have anybody you wish you were rid of?" Naturally your friend does. "The Irish believe there's a way to tell if your wish will ever come true. Want to try it?" Your friend will be curious. Hand her/him a pencil. "Take a sugar cube and print the undesirable's first initial on it—nice and bold." Your friend prints the initial.
2. While your friend is writing, moisten the pad of your right middle finger. You could dip it in a little tea that has spilled into the saucer, or surreptitiously lick your finger. Bad etiquette can be good legerdemain.
3. Take back the pencil and put it away. Now take the sugar cube with the left hand, holding the initial on top, where you can see it. Ask, "Anyone I know?" As your friend answers, take the cube

 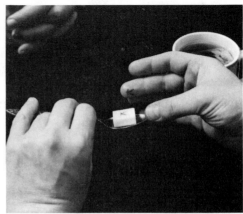

46

between the right fingers, with the thumb below and middle finger above, pressing the pad of the finger firmly against the penciled initial. This imprints a copy of the initial on the skin of your finger. Your left hand now picks up the spoon; your right hand places the sugar cube in the bowl of the spoon; and your left hand places the spoon back on the table.

4. Set the spoon down on the table. Say, "Hold out your hands. Palms down." Your friend does so. Now add, "Identical! Thumbs together!" and, as if correcting his/her position, grasp your friend's hands firmly with your thumbs on top *and your fingers underneath, pressing firmly against the palms.* This transfers a copy of the initial from your right middle finger to your friend's left palm. Pull your friend's hands together, until his/her thumbs touch one another.

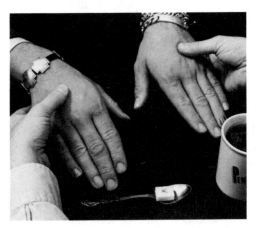

5. Release your friend's hands and say, with great emphasis, "Now you have an important decision to make. Tell me: Which hand do you want to use, left or right?"

a. If your friend says, "Left," say, "Okay, hold your left hand above the teacup and wave it in a small circle." Wait until your friend starts waving the hand. Then add, "Use your other hand to pick up the spoon, and dump your enemy in the tea. Now stir until there's nothing left."

b. If your friend says, "Right," say, "Okay, with your right hand pick up the spoon and dump your enemy in the tea. Now stir until there's nothing left." Wait until your friend starts stirring. Then add, "Hold your other hand above the teacup and wave it in a small circle."

So, no matter which hand your friend "chooses," you interpret his/her answer so that the left hand ends up waving in a small circle over the teacup[1] and the right hand stirs in the sugar. While your friend stirs, softly hum "Danny Boy."

6. When the sugar has dissolved, continue with your instructions: "Take out the spoon and lower your hand. Keep moving it in a circle and feel the steam. Now repeat after me, 'Spirits of the east and west, will I lose this awful pest?'" Your friend repeats the charm. "Now make the Irish gesture of disgust at the teacup, like this..." You make a sharp gesture toward the teacup as if smacking somebody with the back of your hand; your friend copies the gesture, "...and show me the palm of your hand."

7. As your flabbergasted friend shows you the initial on the palm of his hand, shake your head sadly and say, in your best Irish accent, "Hell and damnation! You're *stuck* with the bastard now!"

NOTES

1. This is a superb magic trick. It may read like Dick and Jane, but the effect is truly disturbing. Team up with a friend and learn to perform it perfectly before you try it on a stranger. By the way, this is not a smart trick to explain to your friends. Unexplained it is subtle and eerie. Explained it is simple and dopey. But if you spill the beans to your friends, they won't appreciate its fine points; they'll just make you feel small and rotten.

2. Don't feel obliged to present this as an Irish trick. In reality, it originated with the jadugars of India, those loinclothed street performers who do party tricks to prove their intimacy with Allah. They have a spectator write his name on a stone with the tip of a burnt stick, then heave the stone into the Ganges. Then, asking the spectator to hold out his hands toward the river, the jadugar calls upon his god to preserve the person's name, even though the stone has sunk into the waves. And lo! when the spectator looks at his

---

[1] To be convincing, any occult ritual ought to involve (a) nudity, (b) wearing a bad hat, and (c) assuming an uncomfortable and ludicrous position. We will assume you've gotten (a) and (b) out of the way before you get to messing with sugar-cubes. By making your friend wave a hand over a steaming hot teacup, you achieve (c).

hands, he finds his own name on his own palm in his own handwriting. You can bet the scared spectator forks over quite a few rupees to stay on *that* jadugar's good side.

But the point is: Feel free to adapt this trick to your own ethnic heritage. Penn is descended from Newfoundlanders who are big tea drinkers. He presents this trick as a way his fishermen forefathers whiled away those sixteen-hour winter nights. Teller is one-eighth Cuban. So he does the trick with a cup of coffee and smokes a fat cigar.

HOW TO GET YOUR ETHICAL-VEGETARIAN FRIENDS TO EAT VEAL

Everyone has a price and regular restaurant employees are often damn reasonable. Any cook in a kitchen with a baby cow that's never seen the light of day or walked more than six inches can cut off a bleeding slab, dice it, and slip it into any vegetarian dish.

This trick is just a Gedanken experiment. To really do it would be morally wrong and no challenge. More important, there's no way to make money off it. So, don't do it. But we still couldn't resist putting it in the book.

It's such a good title.

HOW TO GET YOUR CHASSIDIC FRIENDS
TO EAT TREYF[1]

Everyone has a price, but kosher restaurant employees are much too pricey. So the best way to do this trick is with a partner. One partner distracts. (We use either a card trick or naked people performing a live love act. Note that the photo shows a card trick—it's a family book.) The other brings along some pork chops, clams, an octopus, oysters, an eel, a lobster, crabs, a carton of milk, and any carnivorous birds or insects you can get your hands on. (Carnivorous birds or insects? Don't ask us. We didn't make up this list.) Once patrons and employees are sufficiently distracted, dump the above contents into whatever large pot of bubbling kosher food is readily available.

This trick is a Gedanken experiment. To really do it would be morally wrong—and the only challenges are a cheesy card trick and hiding carnivorous insects on your person. More important, there's no way to make money off it, so don't do it.

But we still couldn't resist putting it in the book.

It's such a good title.

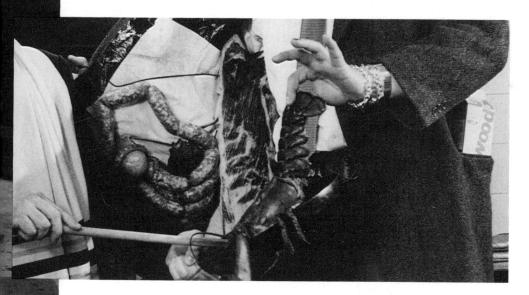

---

[1] Nonkosher

TYING A CHERRY STEM WITH YOUR MOUTH

Subtext, Subtext, Subtext

Tying a maraschino cherry stem in a knot with your mouth is a very sexy thing to do. The manipulation required doesn't really overlap any actual sexual skills, but it certainly demonstrates tongue strength and dexterity and sends the signal to your intended partner that you would like to do with your mouth what she or he does easily with her or his hand. This is sometimes the exact message you want sent.

When you grab your date's cherry stem, saying, "Hey, want to see a neat trick?"[1] you're going out on a limb. Tying a cherry stem with your mouth is a difficult trick. You may fail. Even if you can do it well, you have to think about it too much. You're thinking about the stem when you should be acting the *entendre*. While tying a cherry stem with your mouth, the last thing you want to be thinking about is tying a cherry stem with your mouth. We'll bet you dollars to hot coffee and donuts that when Sherilynn Fenn tied the stem on *Twin Peaks*, she used an edit to switch in a propmaster-tied stem. Sherilynn's a pro, she wants to be able to concentrate on the subtext of the scene, not the gimmickry surrounding it.

Maybe it's important to be completely honest in a sexual relationship, but in dating we need all the help we can get. So when impressing your date by tying a cherry stem with your mouth, you're going to cheat. You're going to switch a previously hand-tied cherry stem for the one you pluck off your date's cherry.[2] And you're never going to 'fess up for the rest of your wretched life.

Here's how you do it:

When you're at a place that serves maraschino cherries, excuse yourself to make a phone call or go to the rest room.

When you're out of sight, get a cherry from the person responsible for the cherry-topped confections or from the bartender.

Using your fingers, tie the cherry stem in a loose knot. It's harder than you think; be thankful you don't really have to use your mouth.

Hide it between the bottom of your lower gum and your lower lip.

Go back to your date. You can sit forever with a tied cherry stem in your bottom lip. You can eat, you can drink, you can talk...you can

---

[1] This is a nerdy way to introduce a sexy trick but very few of us can get away with "Want to see how good I am at oral sex?"

[2] Are we going to be arrested in Broward County? We're just talking about garnishes, we swear.

date, damn it! When the conversation drifts to oral skills (it will), reach over, pluck your date's stem, and casually show your hand empty as you sensually suck the #3 red-dyed stem into your mouth.

Switching the stems in your mouth is easy; don't even think about it. Think about eye contact. Think about your lips. Sense memory, visions of hot, nasty sex should be slow-dancing in your head. (You're kind of on your own here; if we could teach people to be sexy, we wouldn't waste our time writing about tricks with food.) Take a momentary break from the porno in your head and switch the two stems. Use your tongue to pull the tied stem from its hiding place and stick the untied one between your lower gum and lip. If you can't do this, it's just as well—you don't want to get your date's hopes up.

When the sexual tension is ripe, push out the end of the tied cherry stem and have your date gently pull it from between your lips.

Ask "Have you ever seen someone do that?" They probably will say yes—lots of people watched *Twin Peaks* and lots of people do this trick.

Sherrilyn Fenn working[3]

---

[3] See next page.

Okay, so it's not really Sherilynn Fenn. When photo rights get tough, the tough put on lipstick.

Say, "Okay then, I'll do it the hard way." (If you're the kind of person that winks, here's a good place to throw one in.)

Ask your date to loosen the knot a little bit (this is important to the believability) and put the tied stem back in your mouth. (If you can get away with it, give her or his fingers a little kiss as they come to your lips with the stem.)

Keeping sexy acting as your top priority, reverse the two stems again. Take a while on this. Work it. If you make it look too easy, you'll get caught.

Once again, have her or him take the untied stem from between your lips.

Don't be anxious to get the tied stem out of your mouth. You can eat, you can drink, you can even do some making out with the stem hidden. Be patient.

When conversation has moved to other things, bring your napkin to your lips, quietly spit your stem into it, and wad it up.[4]

You can take it from here, babe.

---

[4] Penn decided once to be really slick and swallow the knotted stem, eliminating the evidence. It caught in his throat, causing him to cough, "gack," and choke. This undid any headway the cherry stem trick may have made him. Needing the Heimlich maneuver is not the best way to show your vulnerable side.

THIS IS AS CLOSE TO A FREE LUNCH
AS YOU'LL EVER GET

We made a promise that you would make more than the price of this book back in free meals. It's true. Included in the price of this book is the following great trick to make your friends pay for dinner. We lie and scam for a living, but, in this particular case, you're not the sucker. You bought our book and, in return, we will arrange for your dining partners to buy your meal. That's just the kind of guys we're.

Some of you reading this section haven't bought the book yet. You're standing there by the display and you noticed this chapter advertised prominently; so you decided to sample the merchandise. Look it over. Feel it in your hands. Ask yourself: Is this how I want to spend my hard-earned money? Do I want to learn really cool tricks that will make me a more interesting person? Do I want to be more desirable to the sex or sexes that I find attractive? Do I want a book that will teach me ways to scam free food in an entertaining way?...Huh?...Well?...Okay, freeloading slime, now it's time to stop reading, trot on over to the cash register, and buy your own goddamn copy of *Penn & Teller's How To Play With Your Food*. If you're not going to *buy* our book, why don't you pick up Shirley MacLaine's latest bestseller and paw your greasy hands through that? You'll be able to get the essence of Shirley right here in the store without paying a dime. If you need help: 1. She's a nut. 2. She has too much money. 3. She needs a better hobby. 4. She's unlikely to find a better hobby because...well...she's a nut (see No. 1 above).

Some of the tricks in this book you can learn right away, just by looking at the pictures. You don't have to practice and you don't have to think very much. They're great little tricks but they aren't shoo-ins for free dinner, although they will get you closer to being a great gal or guy that people will *want* to treat. Some tricks in this book have great secrets, secrets that are fun to know. We're sorry, but that's the definition of amateur magic. If the secret is fun to know, then the end user should know the secret. With professional magic, the secret is no fun—it's duct tape (see page 119, step 5), gimmicked props, a confederate, and ugly lies— anything to get the job done. Houdini paid people off. That's showbiz.

This is a professional trick. It's easy, dirty, and will work the first time out. We dined on this, ourselves, until all our friends wised up and insisted on separate checks and a deposit up front. But we worked it for years. Choose your chumps carefully and you'll be able to use it into the next century.

Read the directions, but *pay no attention to the illustrations*. All the illustrations (and captions) on the next two pages are *bogus*. They are intended to mislead semiliterate freeloaders who browse the book in the store and try to steal the valuable information you have paid for. So don't take the pictures seriously unless you want to end up with egg on your face and holes in your wardrobe.

HOW TO GET A FULL COURSE DINNER
FOR THE PRICE OF A TIP

You are at a restaurant with a few friends. You say, "Anybody here want a free meal?" That will get their attention. "Well, we can't all beat the check, but it might be fun to have a little pool. Whoever can come closest to guessing the total bill for food, drink, and tax (not including tip) doesn't have to pay. The others will split the tab."

They will probably reason, "Hmm. If I get lucky, I win big. If I lose, I split the loss with everybody else. Sounds like a good bet to me." It's not. You never get something for nothing; this is axiomatic. If your friends don't know this, soon they will be throwing their hard-earned money away on lottery tickets and horse races. But you can save them from moral and financial ruin by teaching them a lesson.

And all you will charge them for this wisdom is one (or maybe more, if you can get away with it) paltry dinner.

So they agree to try the pool. You give each person a little piece of paper. If you carry business cards, this is a perfect excuse to hand them out. Just be sure that you have a *blank duplicate of whatever you are writing on available for later use.*

Now you tell your friends to write down what they each think the total of the check will be—not including tip. No one may see anyone else's guess. The completed papers are to be folded up and put face-down in front of each person's place.

As the others write their estimates, you do the same. Make your best guess. It doesn't matter at all what you write down—you'll be switching it for the correct answer later. But if you really try to guess, you will *look* like somebody trying to guess, and this little bit of Method acting will make you a more plausible liar.

After all the papers are folded and sitting on the table, order your meal. Have anything you want. This is the time to order double heapin' helpin's of caviar and Lobster Thermidor. Money is no object when someone else is paying. Sit back and just enjoy your meal until dessert

FIGURE 1.

Remove the magnetic stripe from the back of your credit card with sandpaper, and blacken in the area with a felt-tip marker. When you use it at a restaurant, they will think the charge has gone through, but no debit will be made from your account!

FIGURE 2.

As you arrive at the restaurant, find a moment when your date is distracted. Slip all your money into his coat pocket. Then, when the check arrives, show your purse empty and say with anguish, "Oh, no! My money… I must have left it at home…" He has no choice but to be a gentleman and come to your rescue. You've used social pressure to stick him with the check!

◀ **FIGURE 3.**

If someone is engaged in conversation, it is a simple matter to unbutton the pocket with the toes and remove the wallet or money. To make it even easier, cut the toe out of your sock.

and end-of-meal beverages have been ordered. Then glance at your watch, and remark that you have to make a phone call. Excuse yourself and leave the table.

As you move toward the phone, contrive to pass the server and whisper, "Do me a favor, please. Total up the tab and meet me by the telephones. I'll explain later."

When the server shows up with the total, write it on your duplicate card. Or even better, write down an amount close to the total, but a little off; for example, if the real total is $98.22, write $96.75. This makes the punch line more believable (see note 2, page 11).

Tip the server generously (no matter how much you give, it's cheap compared to the bill you won't be paying) and say, "Thanks very much. We'll ask for the check in a few minutes, but please don't tell the rest of my party about our little *rendezvous.*"

Now memorize the total you have written on the duplicate card, fold it to match the card you left at the table, and slip it into your pocket or hold it casually hidden under your purse. Return to the table.

> **TIP: Do not dawdle by the phones. You don't want to give your friends the opportunity to (a) get curious and peek at your "prediction" or (b) figure out some way to cheat _you_.**

Sit down and relax. Enjoy your dessert. Chat. Let a little time and conversation make your friends forget you ever left. Meanwhile, quietly get the duplicate card into your lap. Wait until somebody else remembers the bet. Then say, "Okay, everybody. Let's hear what you guessed. I'll start."

Pick up the card you put on the table at the beginning of the meal and pretend to read it aloud, but really *just recite the amount you wrote down on the duplicate card.* Then in a sentence or two, explain how you "got" your total: "Well, I guessed $96.75 because I figured Valda and Irene would have salads and Sam likes veal and Joe's staying away from high-cholesterol desserts." Note the subtle psychology—at the moment everybody is watching you, you don't do any tricky "moves" at all. You just lie.

Now, to make your lie bulletproof (see pages 43–45), you will switch the card you have misread for the correct one in your lap. You need to get the attention off yourself. So you ask the others in turn to read out the amounts they have predicted and explain their reasoning. And what happens? Attention shifts away from you. So, slowly and casually, you lower your original card into your lap and bring back the duplicate. Do it quietly, without staring at your hands.

Now call over the server and ask for the bill. Have someone read it out. Compare it to all the predictions. Act surprised that you came so close. Then be gracious about your victory. Thank your friends for taking you out to dinner.

As you leave the restaurant, congratulate yourself. You've taught your friends a worthwhile lesson in living, and steered them away from the primrose path to perdition. You've also scammed yourself a grand feed and more than paid for the purchase of this book.

From here on in, pal, it's all gravy.

YEAH, I ATE HALF A ROACH, YOU GOT A PROBLEM WITH THAT?

Teller and I know a lot about cockroaches. To dump the thousand cockroaches on David Letterman's desk we had to become very familiar. We stuck our hands in them, we hid them in our clothing, we cleaned them up. We got used to many varieties from all over the world. We became The Kings of Cockroaches. We built a big part of our career on their hard, shiny little backs.

I felt I had gotten over any disgust that I could feel toward the little buggers. I was wrong. I was in a cheesy Japanese restaurant downstairs from our office in Times Square. I had noodles and a fried chicken thang. I picked up the chicken with my fingers, bit into it, and felt something moving on my lip. My lunch date was Robbie Libbon, the Director of Covert Activities for Penn & Teller, and perhaps the strongest-stomached-Mother-Hubbard-who-ever-ate-scrapple (see page 125). As I felt the movement I looked in Robbie's face and he changed expression. It wasn't much, but it was enough to realize something truly disgusting was going on. I reached up and pulled from my mouth a half-deep-fat-fried wiggling cockroach. Logic tells me it must have crawled into the chicken after it was cooked—but every fiber of my soul tells me that sucker had lived through the fry-o-lator. I threw it down and with batter still attached to its body, and four of its legs crippled, it crawled off under a table.

To my credit, I was able to eat two more mouthfuls (Robbie, of course, didn't forfeit his membership to The Clean Plate Club). To the restaurant's credit, they only charged us for Robbie's meal.

I still eat there.

PSYCHOKINESIS

Using Your Brain to Move a Spoon

In the little packet that came with this book, the Gimmicks Envelope, we gave you a cheap piece of rubber junk from overseas. It's the little rubber bulb with the plastic tubing and the flat rubber bladder and it's called a "Plate-Lifter." It's a great gimmick. It's used to fake psychokinesis. The word "fake" is redundant in that last sentence. As far as we know (and we've looked hard) there is no such thing as "real psychokinesis." No one can move or bend objects with just their mind—unless their mind is living in a brain that's attached to a body that's carrying a wallet that can pay someone else to move or bend the thing they don't want to touch. Or unless that mind can whack the thing in question with a stick.

One reason that some people believe psychokinesis is real is that magicians have come up with lots of ways to fake it, lots of ways for things to "move by themselves." When these effects are done by an entertainer, they yield a cool trick. When done by a scumball, they might be called "psychokinesis."

Enough preaching, let's get to the goddamn trick.

Uncoil the Plate-Lifter. Slip the flat bladder under the tablecloth and lead the tube off the edge of the table and into your lap, where your hand is waiting to squeeze the bulb.

The crudest way to use a Plate-Lifter? Take a plate of sushi. Put it on top of the gimmick, so that the ridge around the bottom rests right on the bladder. Now squeeze the bulb sharply. The plate will jump and the sushi will roll around. Remark, "Jeez, that stuff's *fresh!*" and suck down a tuna roll.

Okay, okay, so far it's not very subtle. Absolutely right. A Plate-Lifter is the kind of gimmick you'd expect to find in a cereal box. But cereal-box gimmicks—with the right Misdirection[1]—have fooled scien-

---

[1] "Misdirection" is magician's jargon for "what you say or do to keep the suckers from thinking of the obvious explanation." (See pages 148–54.)

Here is an opportunity for some serious over-acting.

Cover this hole with your thumb.

We suggest using an opaque plate . . .

. . . and a tablecloth, as well.

The real action is here.

tists.[2] So we came up with a way to use this joke-store junk to perform a world-class con.

Get your Plate-Lifter under the tablecloth with the bulb in your lap, ready to squeeze, and set a plate so that the ridge around the bottom is right on the lifter. Now *slide the end of the bowl of a spoon under the outer rim of the plate*, right next to the lifter. If you squeeze the bulb, it looks as though some invisible force is pressing down on the handle of the spoon[3] and levering up the plate. All your audience's attention goes to the spoon, and the plate will seem incidental—exactly the Misdirection you need to keep from getting busted.

At home, keep the Plate-Lifter under the tablecloth with the bulb hanging ready, where you usually sit. You can remember pretty much where the bladder is and,

---

[2] Scientists are not stupid, but are rarely trained as magicians. This has made for some embarrassing moments where "psychics" demonstrated "phenomena" which scientists eagerly measured and theorized about, only to discover later that they were being conned. Magicians like Houdini, Harry Kellar, and James Randi (see footnote, page 80) have saved scientists a lot of grief.

[3] There *is* an invisible force moving the spoon. It's called gravity.

when you know it's there, it's easy to find. You're always ready. If you're meeting people at a restaurant and you're the first one to arrive,[4] you can slide the Plate-Lifter under the tablecloth right there in the restaurant. If you're really sneaky, you can get it under the tablecloth at a friend's house.

Once you're sitting at a table with your Plate-Lifter in place, and the bulb ready to squeeze, don't rush. Wait until well into the meal. Better yet, wait until after the meal. You don't want anyone to remember that you were the first one at the table. Be cool. When the time is right, turn the conversation to the paranormal, to things "science can't explain." For our taste, it's too easy to get people talking about this nonsense. Let other people do most of the talking. We don't know how much your friends buy the New Age hype but someone should mention "mind over matter," "psychokinesis," or "telekinesis." Have someone explain to you how it works. With amazement in your voice say, "You mean you can concentrate on something and get it to move? Let's try it."

Pick up a middle-size plate and rest its bottom rim on top of the bladder of the Plate-Lifter. Slide the bowl of a spoon under the rim as we explained. Concentrate. Make everyone concentrate. Make them work for it. While they're concentrating, slide the bulb into your hand. Make them keep concentrating. The harder they work on it, the more they'll appreciate it. When everyone is working and concentrating, give a slow squeeze.[5] It'll look like the spoon is moving the plate. Smarter people at the table may check for thread going to the handle of the spoon. They'll find diddly.

That's it. It's amazing. After the miracle, let everyone examine the spoon and the plate. Nothing. Tell them it's not "psychokinesis" but a trick that you did. That way you're not an immoral scumball and, more important, when you say it's a trick, you get all the credit yourself instead of having to share it with everyone that concentrated.

You've done an amazing trick and moved up a notch in your peer group. You only have one problem left: The Plate-Lifter is under the tablecloth and everyone is trying to catch you doing something fishy. Hey, don't worry about it, just leave it. Next time you want to do the trick, buy another copy of *Penn & Teller's How to Play with Your Food* by Penn Jillette and Teller.

---

[4] "To be early is to be on time. To be on time is to be late. To be late is unforgivable." Penn & Teller live by this rule. It's gracious and gives you time to get your gimmicks in place before the others arrive.

[5] Be sure to keep your thumb over the hole in the bulb. (Hey, we told you it was cheap rubber junk.)

Gory special effects celebrate the victory of art over cruelty. Every time a movie monster rips the intestines out of a college student, every time a cinema cop blasts off the back of a gang member's skull, every time a fictitious fiend lops heads off necking lovers, we feel the thrill of a life-and-death struggle without anyone shedding a drop of real blood.

Phony violence helps us live more gently than people in ages past. In old Rome if you needed to get your heart pumping with primal passion, you went to the Coliseum and watched slaves murder each other with pitchforks. In sixteenth-century Europe, you watched savage dogs tear apart wild bears chained to stakes.[1] But today we are much kinder to our fellow man and beast. Nowadays entertainment kills only time.

There's one catch to our preference for special effects over true violence. Trick mayhem is hard to do convincingly. It takes *work* to hide the little blood bags and burst them at just the right moment. Even a simple stunt like "Bleeding Heart Gelatin Dessert" (see pages 104–109) entails quite a bit of preparation. It hardly seems fair that stiffs willing to do homework have all the fun, while lazy slugs miss out.

So for the sluggards we invented this dish.

THE TRICK

You're dining at home. You bring out the bowl of plain cooked pasta. "I seem to have forgotten the sauce!" you exclaim. When your friends look over, you jab your palm with a table knife or fork and stick your hand into the bowl. As they stare appalled, marinara oozes out through the linguini. You stir it in and serve.

SECRET PREPARATION

1. Your secret preparation happens in the kitchen as you are putting the pasta into the serving bowl. It actually entails a bit *less* work than you would have to do if you served the dish normally: You don't even have to stir the sauce in! Let the pasta drain and *cool*. For the trick to work properly it should be cool enough that you can press your palm against it without discomfort.
2. While the cooked pasta is cooling, spoon a big glob of marinara sauce into the middle of the serving bowl (enough to dress the bowlful).
3. Now pick up handfuls of the pasta and gently arrange it around and

---

[1] Bearbaiting. Shakespeare's big competition for the entertainment shilling.

on top of the sauce until there's no longer a trace of red visible. It works best if the layer of pasta directly over the sauce is as thin as it can be and still mask the marinara.

PERFORMANCE

1. Wash your hands. This trick should be unseemly, not unsanitary.
2. Bring out your gaffed dish of pasta.
3. Turn the palm of one hand away from the diners and tap it with the other hand, as if locating a vein. Then pretend to pierce your skin with a table knife or fork. (*Don't* really jab yourself. Achieve verisimilitude, not verity. Remember Sir Larry Olivier's advice to Dustin Hoffman, who had just run several miles in order to look out of breath in a scene in *Marathon Man*: "My dear boy, why don't you try *acting*? It's *so* much easier.")
4. Without revealing your "wound," place your hand, palm down, on the surface of the pasta. Press. Use your free hand to rub your forearm as if stimulating the flow of blood. Keep pressing, until the sauce squishes up through the pasta. A scream of agony enhances the effect.
5. Remove your "wounded" hand from the bowl, keeping the sauce-covered palm away from the guests. Suck the wound noisily, making sure to get plenty of sauce on your chin. Then wipe your hand and face with your napkin. Take a fresh breath, serve the linguini, and wish your guests *bon appétit*.

TOUCHES

1. The purist might want to leave the room after the trick, wash the "injured" hand, and return with bandages across the palm.

2. If you have a favorite pasta restaurant where you are known, tell them how to set this trick up for you. Then, when you come in and order "Linguini—without sauce, please," you can really startle your guests by showing them how you make your own.

3. If the bishop happens to be over for dinner, alter the presentation slightly. Go into convulsions, trembling and crossing your eyes in your best Agnes-of-God-in-Ecstasy fit. Stick both hands into the pasta, "bleed," and pull out your hands with a nice puddle of sauce in the middle of each palm. You'll end up either chastised or canonized.

CREDIT WHERE CREDIT'S NOT DUE

If Columbus could get away with it, why not you?

No, we're not referring to the so-called Columbus egg-balance, in which one takes an egg, stands it on end in a pile of salt, then blows the salt away, except for a few almost invisible grains that hold the egg apparently balanced on end. We're alluding to the secret of Columbus's really big trick: the one that got him the food to stay alive.

The Columbus Egg-Balance.

On his fourth voyage to the New World, Columbus's ships leaked so badly that he got stranded for a year in Jamaica, which would have been a rather pleasant island holiday if his crew hadn't playfully taken to robbing and raping the residents. This made the Jamaicans so grumpy they cut off the food supply to the ships.

Desperate, Columbus thought of a scam to save the day.[1] He checked his handy copy of Regiomontanus' *Ephemerides*, an almanac that contained predictions of eclipses, and found himself in luck. In three days' time, Regiomontanus predicted a total eclipse of the moon. So Columbus sent out a messenger to call the local chiefs to a meeting to be held the afternoon of the eclipse.

---

[1] It was such a neat one that Mark Twain "borrowed" it for his novel, *A Connecticut Yankee in King Arthur's Court.*

When the Jamaican leaders showed up on February 29, 1504, Columbus declared that his god was angry with them for thwarting his holy mission. When they responded with "What a load of plantain pulp," Columbus warned that his god would send an omen that evening at moonrise, a sample of the holocaust to come if they were not cooperative.

That evening, the moon rose, turned red, and disappeared. Suddenly the locals found themselves more inclined to be hospitable to the repulsive foreigner. They converged on his worm-eaten ship with apologies and big trays of hors d'oeuvres. Touched, Columbus retired to his cabin to implore his god to cancel the apocalypse. About forty-eight minutes later (coincidentally the duration of totality) he emerged with the good news that as long as victuals were forthcoming, his wise and powerful deity was willing to forgive. The moon returned, and in their relief none of the chiefs thought to ask why such a wise and powerful deity hadn't just weatherproofed the ships to begin with.

The basic principle—of taking credit for something that happens naturally—is a useful way of getting applause, especially if one has nothing legitimate to offer. It's a favorite of presidents (who attribute booms to executive mandate and busts to legislative folly) and psychics (the goofiest was the one who, when old Big Ben suffered a mechanical failure, got into the news by claiming it was caused by his telekinetic power run amok).

But you too can make use of this time-dishonored principle.

LET US BE YOUR REGIOMONTANUS

We predict that if you drop a plastic pushpin into a glass of soda pop, seltzer, or carbonated mineral water, after a few seconds the pin will stand up on its sharp end, spin like a ballerina *en pointe*, then a few seconds later rise to the surface and float.

We have reasons for this prediction. Fizzy water has a lot of carbon dioxide gas crammed into it. The gas is as feisty as an atheist at a public school prayer rally, and wants to get free—but it's hard to push against all those sanctimonious water molecules and make a bubble to escape in. It needs a head start.

That's where your pushpin comes in. Cheap plastic pushpins have all sorts of microscopic nooks and crannies that the carbon dioxide molecules can lodge in to build bubbles. The scientific term for these locations is "nucleation sites," but just think of these as hidden caves where the rebels gather strength. When the bubbles get big and strong, they act like a life jacket, and lift the pushpin to freedom at the surface.

SO GET TO THE TRICK ALREADY

Okay, here it is.

Pour yourself a glass of fizzy water. Any beverage made from carbonated water will work, from common lemon soda pop to vintage mineral water.

Show your audience a plastic pushpin and drop it in the glass. It will fall to the bottom and remain there for a few seconds (exactly how long depends on the intensity of the carbonation). Before it has a chance to rise, moisten a finger and rub in a circular motion around the rim of the glass, as you would if you were trying to make the glass "sing." Before long (when enough bubbles have formed) the pin will rise and stand balanced on its point. Stop rubbing the glass. Carefully remove your hand, as if the slightest jolt might break the spell. This is just window dressing, but all these touches are what make the trick plausible and good.

Now get dramatic. Stand back. Extend your arm toward the glass. Wave your hand as if directing a stream of magnetic force from your fingers. Soon the pushpin will rise to the surface. Continue to gesture with your hand as you gingerly approach

the glass and pluck the pin from the water. Drop it on the table and fling yourself into a chair, as if exhausted from your effort.

You can repeat this trick (assuming you can muster the energy to "concentrate" again) without fear of detection. As long as you *keep the attention on you*, people will not give a second thought to the water. They will be wondering what your gestures are for, and hypothesizing about static electricity and magnetic force fields. When you finish, hand out the pushpin for inspection, then drink or dump out the glass of water and invite people to examine the glass.

> **NOTE: Don't drink the pushpin. Not only will it kill you, but worse, it will make people think the pin was gimmicked and you have just chosen an eccentric way to keep them from examining it.**

TIPS

1. The slower the action, the more effective the trick. If you get a chance to fool around with your glass of liquid before you start, you will find that by stirring the carbonated water with a spoon for about two minutes you can get rid of a lot of the carbonation, and slow down the process a lot. You will be able to drop the pin in and chat for a while before starting the trick. This will also give you a nice dramatic pause before the final rise.

2. Know your fizzy water. Try the trick with the various soda beverages you tend to encounter, and learn which are the best and how quickly the trick happens in them.

3. The trick is much prettier looking with clear liquids, like seltzer and lemon-lime, than with colas and other colored soda pop.

4. Don't point out that the liquid is carbonated. If it's seltzer or mineral water, refer to it as "water." Act as though the contents of the glass are unimportant—as if you just used the handiest liquid available. That way if your friends try it on their own, they're likely to use plain tap water and fail miserably, even though they "concentrate" themselves blue in the face.

SPOON-BENDING, A REALLY LOUSY TRICK
FOR REALLY LOUSY PEOPLE

You've heard of someone professing to bend spoons with his mind. Some say it's not a magic trick. Well then, it sure is a goofy super power to claim: the ability to do something with supernatural brain energy that no one wants done; and, if they did want it done, they could do it easily with their hands. (There's even a stripper we saw in Vegas who probably could do it with...well, never mind, it's a family book.) If spoon-benders really had psychic powers, we'd all want to sit them down and talk priorities and division of labor. We mere mortals will take care of the necessary cutlery distortion, the *Übermenschen* and *Überfrauen* start setting their superminds to curing cancer and finding cheap renewable sources of energy.

To most people spoon-bending is just a joke, and that's good. Laughing is the best defense against these would-be robbers of human dignity. Laugh right in their faces if you're forced to be that close. Claiming to have powers that don't exist is evil. There's enough trouble figuring out what's going on with our universe without having sand kicked in our eyes. It's a bad thing if some scientists, lacking the specific knowledge and skepticism of conjurers (see note 2, page 67), waste precious brain power on losers whose only marketable skill is exploiting natural human trust. This skill does not require years of careful study; all one has to do is get over the proper moral objections.

The lying we'll be talking about for this specific trick is different from what we call lying elsewhere in the book. In the rest of the book, the use of the word "lie" is gross hyperbole. We use it to describe setting up a joke for a friend, someone whose trust you will still deserve after amusing them with a trick. But real lying is even easier. Once you decide to lie, the only problem is getting caught. Getting caught is often the result of guilt. Get over guilt and lying with a straight face requires less skill than robbing a liquor store with a shotgun.

Unfortunately, the concept of evil genius is part of our culture, the idea that "you gotta admire the skill" of villains. Victims of robbers, people who have had a purse or briefcase stolen, talk about the "precision" and "speed" of the "well-rehearsed" team of thieves. Compare *this* "well-rehearsed, meticulous team" to *honest* people who have really mastered the running-hand-off. Just for fun, let's match this gang of purse-snatching scumballs against an Olympic relay team. Don't make us laugh—we have chapped lips. Giving charlatans credit for skill is like admiring a rapist's proficiency with women: Without the threat of violence the event wouldn't happen. Rapists are not compared to Warren Beatty, Wilt Chamberlain, or John-John.

Guys who do spoon-bending[1] just bend spoons when people aren't looking. It's not difficult sleight of hand. They wouldn't last five minutes at a close-up table with a real technically deft professional like Jamy Ian Swiss or even the hacks at the Magic Castle. It's not acting, acting is harder. You know the actor is playing a part and he or she convinces your heart without insulting your mind. To call it "acting" is to insult Robert De Niro and everyone in his profession. A psychic on a good day couldn't touch Jim Varney on a bad one. Know what I mean, Vern?

So, what's the punch line? Where are we going with this? Well, we wanted to tell you how psychics do spoon-bending, but the tricks are so lousy, they aren't even fun to expose.

But here's a way to bend a spoon just by lying:

1. Convince someone you have real psychic powers. Become their friend. Get them to trust you. This is the most important step. The abuse of friendship and common human trust is the method.

---

[1] In these descriptions, any particular bumbling spoon-bending has-been may pop into your mind. I guess it might be possible that the example you happen to be thinking of might-could-maybe-possibly be the one-in-a-kachillion-outside-chance-of-a-snowball-lasting-a-month-of-Sundays-inside-a-burning-gas-kiln-in-hell be real. We haven't seen every spoon-bender on every second of his or her life. We just haven't seen or heard of one of them doing anything that seemed to us like anything other than bush-league sleight of hand.

We have to be careful though. When these twerps lose their ability to support themselves with public and private "experiments" (they never call them "shows," we guess because they're not entertaining enough), they can decide to turn to litigation. So, let us say right here, Penn & Teller haven't seen or heard about any real psychic spoon-bending, but if we do, we'll happily change our collective mind. We'll want to see it done in front of a panel that is educated in magic, and it should be on videotape and we'd love to see it under oath in a court of law.

Maybe by the time this book comes out some of these swine will have had their days in court and proven they have supernatural powers. We'll be red-faced but we'll admit we were wrong. You may not notice our embarrassment, however, because everyone will be too busy throwing out all scientific knowledge and starting over.

Our lawyer says we need to make it clear that spoon-bending *could* be proven to be a real power.

And maybe that same day Porky Pig will appear incarnate and fly around the courtroom.

Hey man, it could happen.

2. Say you can't work under real test conditions because the skepticism will ruin your concentration.
3. Tell them it doesn't work all the time so you aren't pressured to perform on demand.
4. Wait until they're not looking, ram your thumb into the bowl of the spoon and bend it. If it's a tough spoon, use the surface of a table.

Yup, sorry, that's all that there is to it.

5. Cover the bend with your fingers so they don't know you bent it when they weren't looking.

From here on in, just more lying.

6. Lie about concentrating, lie about energy, lie about being trustworthy, lie about the spoon not being bent already and slowly slide your fingers to reveal the spoon's bend.

Breaking all the known laws of physics.

7. Collect your ill-gotten gains and undeserved respect.

You're a big, important person.

8. Enjoy yourself while you can. Wait until the side of truth and justice makes you the laughingstock.

There will be a name for your pain, "James Randi."[2]

If you want good psychic tricks try the Blister Trick on page 161, the Plate-Lifter Trick on page 66, and the Spoon-Breaking Trick on page 148. You don't want to be a spoon-bender; you don't want Randi and us coming after you to crush you like an insignificant insect.

---

[2] James Randi is the best person in the world. He's a great magician, an inspiration, and a dear friend. Randi's books *Flim Flam!* (Prometheus), *The Truth About Uri Geller* (Prometheus), *The Faith Healers* (Prometheus), and *The Mask of Nostradamus* (Scribners) are required reading for anyone interested in separating lies from facts.

Without Randi, there would not be a Penn & Teller.

He gets sued a lot, so after you've read the books and fall in love with him, you'll probably want to send a few bucks to:

The James Randi Legal Defense Fund
℅ Bob Steiner
P. O. Box 659
El Cerrito, CA 94530

HEADS—I WIN ALL.   TAILS—YOU LOSE HALF.

You wouldn't think a double-headed coin would be any good for getting free meals, would you? After all, instead of betting how the coin happens to fall, you're just betting on whether the mark[1] picks "Heads" or "Tails." There must be a study somewhere that can give you a statistical edge, based on socioeconomic and educational background. But why bother? It's easier than that to cheat.

The trick is to only bet when you're going to win. And that's easy. Carry a double-headed coin (if you want to carry a double-tailed coin, just reverse the following directions—ain't that something?). You can buy a double-headed coin at any magic shop. (And while you're at the magic shop, do us a favor: point to the most expensive thing on the wall and say "Penn & Teller gave away the secret to that the last time they were on TV." It'll make them crazy and it helps keep up our image.)

Every time you go out to eat with one other person, take out your double-headed coin and say, "I'll flip you for the check." Flip the coin in the air and ask them to call it.

If they say "Tails," you let it fall, it's heads and they pay.

If they say "Heads," catch the coin in the air and say, "I just wanted to see if you were a good sport. Let's split it."

A friend of our dear friend, James Randi (see previous page), claims to have done this nearly every time he's gone out to eat since he was a kid. With the "law of very big numbers," he's saved a very big bundle.

Never gamble with any friend of Randi's.

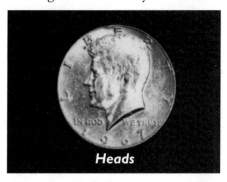

Heads

Tails

---

[1] Carny slang for "appointed victim." When the ticket seller saw a lot of money in the wallet of a patron, he would usher him into the tent with a hand on his back. In the hand was chalk and the "mark" had a mark so the pickpockets would know who to hit while the audience was laughing at the freaks and geeks.

PRACTICAL JOKES AS GENTLE SURREALISM
or
TELL 'EM PENN SAYS HI

"So little of what might happen, does happen."
—SALVADOR DALI

Or something like that. We can't remember which book it's in, but Dali is asking why, when he orders dinner, the waiter doesn't ever bring him a flaming phone book. Sal wanted to live in a wackier world and he helped create one. Dali did goofball art, beautiful, but always wacky, out where the busses don't stop. Many people don't consider him a serious artist. When you use mustache wax, carry a cane, and pose with Alice Cooper and a beer can for a hologram, you run the risk of being considered plebeian. But he's a hero to us.

Practical jokes make a few more of the things that might happen, happen. Lately, we've expanded our idea of what a practical joke can be. We've discovered in the past five years that they don't have to be mean-spirited. Mean ones are still fine, of course: We were proud when we dropped a thousand cockroaches on David Letterman and scared him into leaving the set of his own show. We liked lying about the time on live TV in Times Square on New Year's Eve 1991. But, lately we've been finding senseless, petty generosity even funnier.

I don't remember what we were doing out of the city, but we were in a diner in Jersey about five years ago. There were four of us and we were in a good mood. We were eating classic Jersey diner food. I got onto the subject of red Jell-O.[1] I wasn't saying anything very original, just the usual stuff about how "red" became a flavor as well as a color. I was reveling in the idea of Jell-O. I looked on the menu and a serving

---

[1] "Jell-O" is a registered trademark of General Foods. If it becomes generic through this kind of careless usage of the brand name to mean all gelatin deserts, General Foods will no longer have exclusive use of the name. "Jell-O," like "cellophane," "zipper," "flashlight," "trampoline," "thermos," and "aspirin," will lose its capital letter. It will become property of anyone that feels like adding sugar and food coloring to boiled horses' hooves.

We've been told that if you go to the cafeteria at the "Jell-O" factory, the sign above the "Jell-O" says "Jell-O brand gelatin dessert." "Jell-O," "Band-Aid," "Kleenex," and "Xerox" are fighting the good fight and we sympathize...but the story doesn't read as well with "red gelatin dessert." So, please, as you read on, just keep in mind that Jell-O is one of our many flavored gelatin desserts. (We think Dezerta is another and Knox probably has one too.)

of Jell-O with whipped cream was fifty cents. Wow, cheap. I looked around the diner, there were a couple dozen people. I called the waitress over. "Jell-O for the house."

"What?"

"I'd like to buy each person in this restaurant an order of Jell-O, including you."

"You can't do that."

"What? I figure there are twenty-four people here, I'll give you twenty bucks. That'll cover Jell-O for all the patrons, the staff, and a tip for you."

"We don't allow that."

"You have a rule on this?"

"Yes, we don't allow it."

"Have people tried to buy Jell-O for everyone before?"

"We don't allow it."

She wasn't understanding the joy of Jell-O and it was bumming me out. I hung tough. "Could you check with the manager, please?"

She left and pretended to check. She came back shaking her head, "He says we don't allow it." I was getting mad, but every time I thought of red Jell-O, I was happy again. I decided to scale down. "Could I buy Jell-O for that one guy sitting at the counter?" I pointed to a trucker with his rig parked outside. He was the Yang to the Yin of the truckers in the "Milkshake as Self-Defense" story, page 13 (much of my life has taken place in diners).

"No."

"Aw, c'mon. Please? I'll give you five dollars."

A friend at the table said, "You can't stop him from buying Jell-O for a stranger." I didn't know there was legislation on this, but the waitress bought it.

"Okay, I'll give him Jell-O. But only him. You aren't buying Jell-O for everyone. We don't allow that."

"Not everyone, just him. And tell him Penn says hi." I gave her the five bucks.

Pat, the friend that questioned the legality of stopping a man from buying Jell-O for another man, and I were thrilled to pieces. This was going to be great. The two women at our table, Sarah and Joy, thought the trucker would come over and beat me up.

"You can't beat someone up for buying you Jell-O. What's the crime in that?"

"You can't tell about people," Sarah said, and I immediately started to worry. We watched the Jell-O being delivered across the room. The waitress talked with him as she put the Jell-O down. She pointed at me and he turned around and looked. We all smiled and waved. He didn't smile back, he just looked at me. He tentatively began to eat the Jell-O. We were terrified. Time stood still while we watched him eat. He finished and walked over, his face expressionless.

"Are you Penn?"

"Yes, I am."

"Did you buy me Jell-O?"

"Yes, I did."

"Why'd you do that?"

"I was thinking about how much I liked red Jell-O and how funny it would be to buy some for a stranger."

He broke into a smile. "That's great. I haven't had Jell-O since I was a kid. It's really great. I never even think about eating it, let alone buying it for someone else. Do you do this for a lot of people?"

"No, this is the first time."

"What made you think of it?"

"I don't know, it just popped into my head."

"It's a great idea. I'm going to start buying Jell-O for strangers. It seems like fun."

"Really?"

"Yup. I'll tell them Penn says hi."

"Thanks."

I've done it since. But, let me tell you, the first time is the best. Some day, I may get the nerve to have a waiter bring a flaming phone book to a strange artist.

FEAR, DAMAGE, HOUDINI, DROWNING, GLORY, AND THE GREAT EGG DROP

Certain things used to make me sick. The thought of leeches clinging to my flesh, for example, or live rats crawling across my face. I used to jump when a roach ran out from under the stove, and I got a little unsteady at the sight of my own blood.

Irrational fears, all of them. Leeches are not dangerous or even particularly painful. Rats couldn't care less about the face they're walking on. Roaches neither bite nor carry disease.[1] And cuts heal, leaving attractive scars to advertise one's *machismo*.

On the other hand, *sensible* fears are worth having. It pays to unplug the toaster before cleaning it. But where do you draw the line between fears that keep you safe and fears that keep you from having fun? We have a quick, sure guideline we follow whenever we have to make this decision. It's a rule that's long been popular in the S&M set but deserves a wider audience.

It's the principle of No Permanent Damage.

You want your life to be full of zing. You want adventure, thrills, and a reputation for being a nut. But you don't want to lose an eye. You don't even really want to break a leg (it might heal improperly and bug you when it rains). NPD is the perfect place to draw the line. Before you start any daring enterprise, ask yourself, *Am I exposing myself to any possible damage that would harm me for life?* If the answer is no, then you know you are safe to give it a whirl.

Just about everybody who has a reputation for being larger than life has used this rule. Look at Houdini.

Harry would get shackled with dozens of handcuffs and leg irons. Then he'd be nailed into a packing crate and dumped off a dock into the sea. Just when everybody had given him up for dead, he'd burst to the surface, wave and pose for pictures. When the headlines came out in the next day's papers, a few thought he was a suicidal crackpot who got lucky, but most thought him a god.

He was neither. He was a meticulous devotee of NPD. At every step

---

[1] When Penn auditioned for John Schlesinger, the director of *Marathon Man* (see page 70), Schlesinger asked if he was bothered by cockroaches (see page 65). Penn asked him how *he* felt about dentists. This led to a good conversation about how it's easier to scare someone else with something that scares you. Penn felt he had a lot in common with Schlesinger, and Schlesinger was very nice, but he still gave the part to someone else—the rat-bastard.

along the apparently hazardous way, he would make sure the bottom line was covered.

Houdini was *the* expert on locks. He could tell at a glance if a set of cuffs or shackles might give him problems. So he started off by specifying that he would escape from any "standard" manacles. That way, whenever he spotted a lock that would take too long to pick, he could sneer "Nonstandard!" and throw it aside. With the clock of life and death ticking he refused to gamble on an unknown.

But what about the box he was nailed into? You would read that it had been built by the local carpenters' union. You'd get the impression that they showed up at the wharf with a crate Houdini had never seen before and sealed him inside however they pleased. And that's just what Houdini wanted you to think. The press rarely mentioned that Houdini often helped design the "challenge" box, always inspected it, and sometimes even had his staff transport it from the shop to the waterfront—in an enclosed truck where they could make last-minute "improvements" to ensure the maestro wouldn't get stuck.

But when they threw the box off the dock, how come Houdini never got knocked unconscious? Because the box was never thrown. It was lowered slowly and dramatically on ropes from a big, secure crane. And by the time they had nailed, roped, and lowered the box, Houdini had all the handcuffs and leg irons off and was ready to make his exit. He was always one step ahead.

But what if something went wrong? Well, if you study the old photographs of the crowd anxiously awaiting the outcome, you'll notice a few faces that show up again and again. Those are Houdini's buddies, lounging inconspicuously among the crowd, quietly checking their watches, just in case the boss doesn't pop up on cue and they have to kick into the emergency rescue plan.

Now, I'm not telling you all this to make Houdini seem less cool. No matter how cautious his planning, it still took nerves of steel and fantastic strength, agility, and breath control to submit himself to chains, cramped boxes, and icy rivers. He had to learn to work under conditions of pain and terror that would paralyze most people. But knowing how to use the rule of NPD, Houdini could distinguish between dread and danger. It gave him the power to drive his audiences crazy with tension and mystery—and live to take the applause afterward.

NPD is a rule that can make even wimps look heroic. Take me, for example. I'm no daredevil. I never speed on the highway, because I once got a speeding ticket and had to go to those compulsory classes where they spend eight hours showing you colorful pictures of dead speeders. I wash my hands a lot to keep from catching colds. I never stand on the top rung of the ladder.

But in 1985 Penn and I got the chance to be on *Saturday Night Live* for the first time. Lorne Michaels, the producer, had landed as host Madonna, the (at the time) platinum-haired queen of the media darlings. The ratings were expected to go through the roof—far and away the largest audience we had ever played for. It was by anybody's standards a "big break." So we wanted to do something people would really remember. We decided to stick me in a big phone booth full of water, held down under the surface with bars. Penn was to lock me in and not let me out until he had successfully found a selected card. Then he was to miss the card and keep missing until I drowned. We didn't *really* want to drown me—a "big break" is more rewarding if you live through it—so we figured out a sneaky way to make it seem as though I drowned without requiring lung pumps and CPR.

The problem was, there was very little time to prepare the bit, and our clever idea—for keeping me under water longer than the biggest-lunged Samoan who ever dived for pearls—sometimes failed. We worked literally day and night, but there just wasn't time for enough R & D to make sure it would work every time.

So we covered ourselves with a bottom-line precaution: In the event of an emergency I would open and close my left hand rapidly, finger by finger, like an octopus hailing a cab. Marc Garland (see page 41), at the time our Director of Covert Activities (see page 118 for job description), would be watching that hand from off camera. If he saw the "octopus" gesture, he would rush in, unlock the tank, and save me. And if there was some problem with the lock, Marc would open the big valve by the bottom of the tank and spew half a ton of water onto the studio audience. It wouldn't be pretty, but it would beat drowning.

Saturday came much too quickly. We had our camera rehearsal (the trick worked!), and then at 10 P. M. the "dress rehearsal" before a live audience (yippee, it worked again!). Afterward the whole cast and crew assembled in producer Lorne Michaels's office for notes. Lorne suggested one change: Where we had originally intended to leave me dead in the tank, Lorne reminded us that *SNL* was comedy, and that not everybody thought death was as funny as we did. So it was important, he argued, to let me come back to life for a bow at the end. At first we were afraid we'd be wimping out, but we persuaded ourselves that since the viewers at home would know I wasn't really dead, it would be neat to let them know that *we* knew that *they* knew. And we could always tell them later in a book that Lorne was the wimp.

The show began. About an hour into the show, stagehands rolled the half-ton phone booth full of water into place. At the start of the commercial break preceding our spot, I climbed a ladder and lowered myself into the tank. Marc clanged the bars closed over my head. Marc passed me the SCUBA regulator (we started with me breathing from an air hose that Penn ripped out of my mouth when he began the card trick).

One minute to broadcast.

Marc stood in front of the tank and waited for the signal that I was okay. And then I noticed it.

A problem. A small one. But one which, during the seven-minute duration of the trick, could easily become fatal. I won't specify exactly what it was (we have the reputation for giving away how we do all our tricks, but, like so much else we do, that's a lie). Suffice to say, I was in a claustrophobic death chamber with one tricky way to stay alive, and that was starting to fail. So I had to choose:

I could make the octopus gesture and get out immediately. That would save us from humiliation on national television. It would also throw away our first big break on *SNL*. Or I could gamble that we would get through the trick before the problem forced me to give the rescue signal.

Now I'm no macho type. But I know the rule of NPD. So I figured: What was the worst thing that could happen? I'd have to give the octopus signal in the middle of the performance, Marc would rush in and let me out, and we'd look like idiots. But embarrassment does not come under the category of Permanent Damage. Drowning, ripping out your tongue with a corkscrew, that's Damage. But two bozos blowing a trick for an audience of umpteen skidillions? That's just good TV.

So when Marc raised his eyebrows, asking for the go-ahead, I placed the tip of my index finger to the tip of my thumb in the SCUBA divers' international code for "OK."

If you ever see a rerun of that show, you'll notice that every time they cut to a close-up of me in the tank, I looked petrified.

No acting there. My lungs were tightening, and I was staying just as still as I could to conserve the oxygen and avoid aggravating the secret problem, which was growing worse moment by moment. I was thinking, *Please, Penn, don't be too funny. Laughs take time.* And when they ran up and released me at the end of the trick, the expression of joy and relief on my purple face was 100 percent genuine. I could not have stayed under even five seconds longer. All I could think was, *Thank you, Lorne, for making us wimp out.*

The trick was a huge hit. Our raving incompetence passed for heroism. And all because, under pressure, we remembered the rule of No Permanent Damage.

Which brings us to the "Great Egg Drop."

Not every reader of this book will try this trick. But then, not every reader of this book deserves to be an object of peer worship. Some will look at the photos that follow and say, "I can't do that! I'd be crazy!" Such Milquetoasts deserve obscurity.

But the bold reader, the one with a lust for life and the courage that led our species to rule the planet, will consider the bottom line: *Will this do permanent damage? Will my life end if I splatter the dining room with raw eggs and smashed glassware?*

She/he will cast off the chains of cowardice and follow these nine steps to peer-group immortality:

1. Find four tall twelve-ounce tumblers. Arrange them in a square on the table. Fill them each three-fifths full of water.
2. Find a tray with a lip. Make sure the bottom is smooth. Place it on the tumblers. If you are right-handed, let a little extra tray extend to the right (see photo). If you are left-handed, let it hang out a bit to the left.
3. Roll four playing cards into cylinders about three inches long by three quarters of an inch in diameter (i.e., roll them the long way; see the photo[2]). Secure the cards with rubber bands.
4. Stand each cylinder *directly above the middle of a glass supporting the tray.* Do not be casual about this. The position is crucial.
5. Place, pointed end up, an egg on each rolled card.
6. Steady your nerves and take a deep breath.
7. Place your palm against the middle of one side of the tray. Now draw it back about a foot winding up for a swing. Do this twice to build suspense, perhaps chatting between, to give people a chance to get really nervous.
8. Then on the third time, whack the middle of the edge of the tray sharply with your palm, shooting it horizontally across the table. A sharp, short smack is what you want. If you lose your nerve and hit it too gingerly, the tray will not get out of the way of the falling eggs. If you follow through on your swing too much, you will end up shopping for glassware and mopping the floor.
9. If you have done all correctly, the eggs will drop neatly into the glasses without breaking. There will be some splats of water on the tablecloth and a roomful of awestruck admirers. If you have hesitated, followed through too much, or placed the cards wrong, your friends will be dripping with egg and your host will be sending you the dry-cleaning bill. But in either case, you will be alive, and there will be No Permanent Damage.

---

[2] You may notice that on the cover we have deliberately rolled the cards *the wrong way* to mislead the casual browser (see page 59). We think of everything.

TIP #1: *Don't think about the eggs. Concentrate on knocking the tray off without bashing into the glasses.*

TIP #2: *If you have trouble with tip #1, try knocking the tray off the top of the glasses without the eggs in place first. But if you have to resort to this, for goodness' sake do it where people can't see you. Gods are never seen practicing.*

TIP #3: *Make sure nobody's in the way of the tray as it flies out. You'll get a lot less applause if your audience is distracted by somebody groaning and clutching his/her broken windpipe.*

If you have succeeded, you will possess a tool of great power. Not only will you be a celebrity at parties, but you'll find that you can use this trick to support virtually *any* claim about yourself. For example, if a crackerjack tennis player has just challenged you to a game and you want to get out of it, you need only say, "You know I had a Himalayan tennis master who would not let me serve for five years, until I mastered this..." Then you do the Great Egg Drop. Your rival's jaw hits the floor. You continue, "Yes, it took me five years of meditation and precision power training, but since then, I've never had a serve that didn't score. So I just can't get excited about playing anymore."

If you have failed to execute the Drop it may be a few months before your host invites you back. You will, however, have left a memory that will live forever among your peers.

But if you put this book on the shelf without daring, you will suffer the oblivion your crawling cowardice deserves.

The choice is yours. Will you reject glory and adventure like a bug reflexively fleeing from the light? Or will you dare to be worthy of the name *homo sapiens* and snatch at the rapture of life with the palm of your hand and a third of a dozen eggs?

POPCORN

Teller and I like scary movies. We love them. When there's a "cat scare,"[1] a big "boo" surprise that turns out to be something harmless like a kitty, Teller and I jump out of our seats. Teller even screams a little. We're embarrassing to be with at monster and slasher movies. They work on us.

I used to be a lot worse. Until I was twenty-four, I avoided horror movies. I was dragged to see *The Exorcist*. I was living with a woman who was going to college and we didn't have a car. We had to hitchhike back to her place. At the opening credits, I was shook; after standing in the dark on the side of the road and riding home with a stranger, I was useless. As we got to the top of her apartment stairs, her roommate's boyfriend, hiding in the dark, said "Fuck me" in a low Mercedes McCambridge voice.

In fear, I screamed, jumped straight in the air, and grabbed my ankles. There are things about evolution that baffle me. I understand why screamers in panic situations might help the tribe to be the fittest, but where the hell did my jump-in-the-air-and-grab-your-ankles genes come from? What chromosome was that riding on? What prehistoric weakling took a dip in my gene pool? Were cowardly guys with broken kneecaps desirable to Cro-Magnon chicks? I don't get it.

I came down hard on my knees and hit my face against the floor. I was 220 pounds of trembling flesh, crying on the floor. I didn't sleep a wink that night. I just sat in their well-lit living room and listened to insipid Beatle tunes with Ace bandages (see page 82) on my knees and Band-Aids (see page 82) on my face. It was a great joke.

When I was twenty-four, I decided that not seeing monster movies was a character flaw—"Ignorance of your culture is not considered cool."[2] I started seeing them all and I toughened up. George Romero is now my second favorite director. I can watch anything and when I get home I can sleep. But I still jump during the movie; that's part of the fun.

If you know someone that's jumpy in scary movies, here's a gag that works pretty well:

---

[1] Rich Nathanson came up with the term "cat scare" and he can name seventeen literal "cat scares" from *101 Dalmations* to *Alien*.

[2] 1978 promotional poster for *Duck Stab* by The Residents.

1. Get them to go with you to a spooky movie. I suggest using the "bait and switch" method: Tell them you're going to see some Lawrence Kasdan piece of garbage and switch at the last minute. If you can choose a movie with creepy-crawlies, that's the best. Something real buggy like *Arachnophobia* is perfect.

2. Get a large popcorn to share (you can probably make the chump pay for it using one of the other scams in this valuable and surprisingly well-written book).

3. Get a moment alone to do your secret preparation. If your friend runs to the bathroom right before the flick, fine. If not, you can say you're going to the rest room and set it up in the back of the theater.

4. Carefully rip a hole, the size of your wrist, in the side of the bag or the bucket. If you do this carefully, very little popcorn will fall out. Even if many kernels fall to the floor, don't sweat it; "large" in movie popcorn means large. You have plenty.

5. Work your hand into the hole up to the wrist. It looks great, it looks like you're just holding the popcorn.

6. If your friend is sitting on your right, put your left hand in the popcorn and vice versa.

7. Watch the movie and wait as the popcorn gets eaten down to just above the buried hand. Meanwhile the movie gets your fish freaked.

8. Be patient, wait until they go for the perfect scared, distracted, handful of consoling salty, greasy carbohydrate. When his/her hand starts digging around— Grab! Hard! Don't let go! Clamp on! Fight!

They'll go crazy. I don't know what the victim thinks is happening. Maybe they think it's a monster in the popcorn or maybe they think the popcorn has come alive. But whatever they think, they'll be tortured and you'll have a good laugh. If you're lucky, when you let them go, they'll jump up and grab their ankles.

* * *

P.S. Anyone who finished high school will recognize the ancestry of this trick. We asked people we knew if they had ever really tried the slightly different hole-in-the-*bottom*-of-the-popcorn-trick. They had all heard of it, but no one had done it or had it done to them.

So, I tried it.

It works well.

And you don't need a scary movie.

But you don't really need directions for that one...this is a family book.

WARNING WARNING WARNING

The next two pages (100 and 101) look as if they came from a nice Americana cookbook. They didn't. They are a malicious prank. If you follow the recipe, you will just make a mess.

Remember making a "volcano" in elementary school by mixing vinegar and baking soda?[1] Well, on the next two pages, we have disguised that classic chemical reaction as a recipe. We've thrown in egg, milk, and sugar and we've used lemon juice in place of vinegar to make it look more plausible. Then we've spruced it up with cookbooky lingo and prissy little design motifs. Anyone who tries to make Swedish Lemon Angels will end up with a kitchen counter full of lemon-egg foam ten seconds after completing step #4.

How you choose to use this "recipe" depends on your aims and scruples:

1. Use it to solve a social problem. Your friend Marge is always asking casual questions about your secret family recipes. To put her off you have been saying, "One of these days, Marge, I may break down and share that recipe with you." But you don't really want to betray the family heritage. So you copy out *our* recipe on a little file card, renaming and adapting it to fit whatever Marge is dying to know. Age it by dipping it in weak tea and letting it dry so that it looks like Granny's own.

Bring it to work and let it lie casually on your desk, and call Marge over and ask her a question. Watch as her beady, prying eyes spot the recipe. Watch as she strains to keep up the conversation, all the while knowing the precious information is just a glance away. Finally, find an excuse to turn your back or leave your desk for a moment or two. Greedily, she will memorize the recipe as quickly as she can.

Leave her just enough time to study it, but not enough time to write it down. This way, when she goes home in the evening and tries it in the kitchen and gets egg *frappe* all over everything, she will blame it on her memory. She can't ask you what went wrong. That would betray the fact that she snooped. She can't suspect you were setting her up; she thinks *she* was taking advantage of *you*. Her only possible conclusion is that *she forgot some key detail*.

Repeating this every few weeks will drive her over the edge. Each time she will be sure she has it right this time. Each time she will fail, throw the mess in the

---

[1] Baking soda is sodium bicarbonate. The vinegar liberates the carbonate radical and suddenly you have a gush of CO_2 bubbles, which to an elementary school teacher resemble lava.

garbage, and curse herself. You will detect her losing interest in life. To enhance the effect, now and then bring in a fresh batch of whatever she's dying to know about, and offer her one during coffee break.

2. You may wish to use this recipe as a teaching tool. For example, cooking demands much more concentration than non-chefs know. Jimmy likes to come into the kitchen and interrupt when you are measuring ingredients. He asks, "Hey, where's the turpentine?" You answer. Suddenly you are not sure whether you put in five teaspoons of baking soda or six. The biscuits come out as flat lumps of mud. You've asked Jimmy not to interrupt you, but he forgets. You want to engrave your point in his memory.

So you set this book in your clear acrylic cookbook holder, open to pages 100 and 101. As long as Jimmy doesn't see the cover, it looks just like a typical family cookbook, complete with cute motifs. Call him into the kitchen. "Jim, could you do me a favor? I really want to make these Swedish Lemon Angels for dessert, but I've got to find out why my checkbook isn't balancing, and the bank's going to call any minute now. Would you just throw it together? It's an easy recipe. I'll just work here at the table in case you need any help."

As he starts to measure the baking soda, say, "Jim, how much is $121.16 plus 5% of $8.50 minus $49.86?" If he is a savant, he will answer instantly.[2] Otherwise he'll tell you where he left the calculator and turn back to his measuring. In either case he will momentarily lose track of his cooking. He will look from the spoon to the box of baking soda and back again. He will stare into the bowl trying to count the individual piles of baking soda dissolving in the mixture.

When he mixes it all together—voilà Vesuvius! Say, as if consoling him, "Sorry. I must have distracted you. One extra spoonful and the whole thing is ruined." Let him draw his own conclusions. Then ask him to be a sweetheart and clean up the mess.

3. You may wish to spread havoc randomly by fax. Your friend Cyndi has programmed her fax machine to auto-dial thirty friends. Every time she finds a quirky story in the newspaper (**STATUE OF LIBERTY TURNS GREEN—SCIENTISTS MYSTIFIED**) she sticks it in the machine and sends it out to everybody. Many of her friends do the same thing, so that any missive moves to a wide, international audience at the speed of light (actually, at 9600 Baud). Fax Cyndi the recipe. For maximum plausibility, photocopy pages 100 and 101, then add marginalia or a little clip-on note as a personal touch. Pop it in the document-carrier of someone else's fax machine (it's a virus) and send it to everyone on the auto-dialing list.

Within hours, there will be little volcanos erupting in kitchens all over the world.

---

[2] $71.73, rounded up from 71.725, but that's not important.

at 300 degrees for twenty minutes. Cool on a wire rack and store in layers on waxed paper in a tin or wrap individually with plastic wrap.

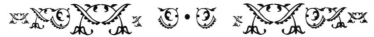

These crisp, airy lemon treats are perfect for holidays, picnics, and that special birthday lunch. As they bake, the lemony smell will fill the house and have the small-fry lining up in advance. This recipe makes eighteen delicate angels.

Swedish Lemon Angels

1 egg
1/2 cup buttermilk (*or* 1/4 cup milk mixed with 1/4 cup vinegar)
5 tsp. baking soda
1/2 tsp. vanilla
1 cup lemon juice (fresh is best)
1-1/4 cups sugar
7/8 cup all-purpose flour
8 tbs. butter or margarine, melted

PREHEAT OVEN TO 375 DEGREES.

1. In a *small* bowl or 2-cup measuring cup, beat the egg until foamy.
2. Add the buttermilk and the vanilla and blend well.
3. Add the baking soda, one teaspoonful at a time, sprinkling it in and beating until the mixture is smooth and the consistency of light cream.
4. Add the lemon juice all at once and blend into the mixture. Stir, do *not* beat (you want it creamy but without a lot of air).
5. The mixture will congeal into a pasty lump. Scoop it out of the bowl using a spatula and spread it on a floured surface.
6. Sift the flour and 3/4 cup of the sugar together and use the fingertips to work it into the egg-lemon mixture.
7. With a floured rolling pin, roll the dough out 1/32" thick, and with the tip of a sharp knife, cut the "angel" shapes and twist up the edges to form a shell-like curve about 3/8" high. Sprinkle on the remainder of the sugar.
8. Brush each "angel" with melted butter.
9. Place angels one inch apart on an ungreased baking sheet and bake for 12 minutes or until golden.

GLOWING PICKLE
(See pages 157–58)

See pages x–xi

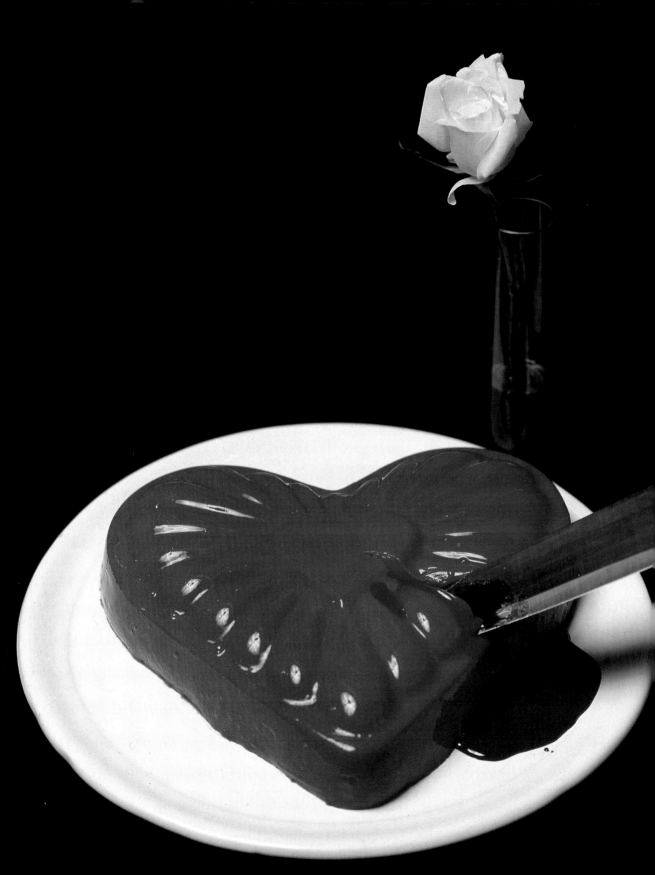

BLEEDING HEART GELATIN DESSERT

The title says it all. It's the perfect *coup de grace* for your intimate dinner at home. As your guests sip their coffee, you unveil a glistening pink gelatin heart on a pedestal cake stand. Then you whip out a carving knife and stab it. Dark, gooey blood issues majestically from the wound. You cut dainty slices off the lobes of the heart and flip them onto dessert plates. You hold each portion under the oozing gash until it is nicely sauced with gore, add a dollop of whipped cream, and serve.

INGREDIENTS

4 cups water
12 oz. (four 3-oz. boxes or two 6-oz. boxes) of peach (pink; think of lung tissue) or strawberry (redder; think of livers and hearts) gelatin dessert[1] mix.
4 envelopes unflavored gelatin
one 12-ounce can unsweetened evaporated milk
1/2 cup grenadine syrup
1 cup light corn syrup (light)
one small bottle(.3 fl. oz.) red food coloring
3 drops blue food coloring
one 1-gallon food-storage bag (the plain kind without the zip closure)
6 1/2 cup heart-shaped gelatin mold or cake pan[2]

PREPARATION

1. Boil the water. Put the packaged gelatin dessert and unflavored gelatin in a bowl and pour the boiling water over it, stirring constantly. Cool to room temperature (very important or the next step may present problems). Stir in the condensed milk. Note how it already is acquiring the color of freshly skinned flesh.

---

[1] We developed this with Jell-O brand gelatin dessert, Knox unflavored gelatin, Carnation unsweetened condensed milk, Karo syrup, Rose's grenadine, and Baggies food-storage bags. This is not product placement—we haven't received truckloads of free Jell-O; it's our attempt to use ingredients we know people can find easily in grocery stores everywhere. This is not to say that we'd reject any research and development supplies the abovementioned companies might graciously bestow now that we've given them such a big plug.
[2] These are especially plentiful around Valentine's Day; the one in the photographs was, at the time of this writing, available from Conran's and Williams-Sonoma.

2. Pour the mixture into the gelatin mold. Cover the bottom of the mold (this will be the top when you serve it) with a layer about half an inch thick. Refrigerate until it gels firmly.

3. Meanwhile, prepare a nice bladder of blood. Stir together the corn syrup, grenadine, and food colorings (we do it right in the measuring cup to save dish-washing—every erg saved in preparation is an erg one can use to enjoy the Payoff). For the bladder (the bag that keeps the blood together inside the mass of gelatin) take the gallon-size food-storage bag and *turn it inside out.* Pour the blood mixture into one corner of the bag and twist it  closed so that no air bubble is caught between the sauce and the twist. Tie a knot in the twisted plastic. Adjust the position of the knot so that when the bag lies on the counter, it's about $1\frac{1}{2}$ to 2 inches high, and tighten the knot. With a pair of scissors, snip off the frilly extra plastic outside the knot.

4. When the gelatin on the bottom of the mold is stiff and firm, position the bladder of blood in the mold, with the point of the bag just inside the point of the heart. *Make sure there is at least 3/4" of space between all sides of the bag and the walls of the mold* (this will ensure that your guests don't see clues ahead of time). Pour in the remaining gelatin until the mold is as full as you can handle. Don't

worry if you see a little of the blood-bladder grazing the surface of the gelatin, as long as it doesn't project too much; the side you are looking at now will be the bottom when you serve it.

5. Refrigerate until gelled firmly to the texture of fine, lean organ meat. It takes about 4 hours.

6. To unmold, put about 2 1/2 inches of hot, but not boiling, water in your sink. Set your mold in the water so that the water comes just below the edge of the mold for 15 or 20 seconds; the time depends on the thickness of the mold pan. Remove the mold from the water, and run the blade of a knife around the edge of the gelatin. Invert your serving platter, ideally a white pedestal cake plate, on top and hold it firmly in place. Then use both hands to turn over the mold and the plate. Remove the mold; you may need to tap or shake the mold slightly to free the gelatin.

PRESENTATION

The blood looks prettiest when it flows over white plates, doilies, and table linen, which it may stain permanently—but what the hell, it's the *effect* that matters. To serve, use a nice, big *Psycho*-style chef's knife and stab the side of the gelatin about one third of the way up from the pointed end of the heart. Twist the knife slightly, and blood will start to ooze out. Bare your teeth like a Marine jabbing with a bayonet, and widen the wound. When the blood is coming at a good clip, grab a dessert plate, and cut a slice from one of the lobes of the heart. Flip it onto the plate, and drizzle it with blood by holding it under the edge of the pedestal. Add whipped cream and serve.

This dish delights all five senses:
1. Sight: red, glossy, and elegantly surreal when the blood starts to flow.
2. Taste: sweeeet.
3. Smell: classic artificial-fruity.
4. Touch: cold and wiggly.
5. Hearing: the screaming of guests.

A NOTE ABOUT SAFETY: Be careful not to serve pieces of the food-storage bag to your friends. They could choke to death. We want to help you become a more exciting host, not a criminally negligent klutz. If, on the other hand, you're deliberately trying to murder your guests, please think up your own modus operandi. Don't try anything that might implicate a couple of innocent fun-book writers.

PIXAR'S LISTERINE HACK

To computer people, scams, practical jokes, and most anything sneaky and clever are "hacks." Our computer buddies congratulate us on our "Letterman hacks." This book could be called "Penn & Teller's Food Hacks."

Pixar is a company in Northern California that does computer animation. Their animation includes stuff like "Luxor Jr.," "Knick Knack," and the Academy Award winner, "Tin Toy." These guys kick ass and take names. I don't really remember when we first met them, but when we're playing San Francisco, we make time to hang.

Pixar does computer animation for TV commercials and they had the Listerine account. They did the groovy advertisement of the Listerine bottle boxing. It's a good-looking ad. Working on that commercial brought them in contact with the Listerine advertising agency. They got an idea for a hack.

Everybody knows that Listerine has a chemical in it that makes you vomit[1] if you swallow too much of it.[2] The thinking is: Because Listerine is 26.9% alcohol, they put this magic chemical in so they won't get a bad reputation from drunks swilling it down. (We like this idea. We wish Dom Perignon and Budweiser were as considerate of our civilization.)

On the day of a big Listerine meeting the Pixar guys—John, Craig, Flip, and Andrew—got two big bottles of Listerine. (They didn't have to go far. They had cases lying around for modeling purposes.) They opened one bottle and left it open in the room—allowing that distinctive Listerine smell to waft.

They took the other bottle, emptied it out, and rinsed it out a few times. Even rinsing the bottle several times, that smell still lingers. They

---

[1] In this story we will refer to vomiting several times. The temptation to use a different euphemism or dysphemism at every junction is overwhelming. But, since President Bush had his embarrassing incident in Japan, it seems we've heard everything from "technicolor yawn" to "calling Ralph on the porcelain phone" one too many times. We'll stick to "vomit," "barf," "throw up," and "puke."

[2] This is what Pixar told us; we had never heard this "fact." It turns out that like many things "everybody knows" this seems to be false. We called Nancy Fitzsimmons, who does P.R. for the Warner-Lambert Co. (they own Listerine), and she said there was no special chemical in Listerine to make you vomit. I guess it just tastes bad enough that it's easy for everybody to believe there's a chemical in it to make you puke.

mixed apple juice and water in the gaffed[3] bottle to match the Listerine color in the reference bottle. They screwed the top back on tightly.[4]

That's all. They were set. When the meeting started, random-chance-in-a-godless-universe smiled on our heroes. The producer of the Listerine spot, who was *not* in on the gag, mentioned the "fact" about the anti-wino-barf-chemical (do winos even mind barfing?) in the Listerine. They pounced. Flip eyed the bottle. John pulled out a twenty-dollar bill and threw it on the table. He dared Flip to drink the mouth-wash "just down to the top of the label." Andrew matched the twenty bucks.

Flip picked up the bottle and took a deep breath. Stopping to breathe between each slug, he drank down to the top of the label. He acted up a storm, the smell filling the room. The Suits were turning green. Flip was trying for his first nonanimation Academy Award. When he'd killed it to the label, Craig offered him another $20 to polish it off. Judi, the producer from Listerine, had to leave for the rest room where she threw up from Flip drinking *apple juice*.

A perfect hack.

In the classic "that was awful—let's do it to someone else," Judi had them set it up a couple weeks later and swilled it herself to freak out her bigwigs.

---

[3] Carny/magician slang for gimmicked, rigged, not on the up and up.

[4] Let this be a lesson to you. Companies like Warner-Lambert put seals on their products for a reason. Always check the safety seal before an important bet.

BE PICASSO, NOW, WITHOUT TALENT

Picasso's art kills us dead. But one way he used his art kills us even deader: Picasso would sometimes pay for meals with a little sketch. Can you beat that? Way beyond cool. The one downside was he really wasn't ripping anyone off. The restaurant people got to enjoy their own original Picasso (or if they needed the money they could sell his little drawing for much more than the cost of a meal). And if they did hold on to it, they could end up damn rich. It was a good deal all around.

Imagine being Picasso, finishing a meal, making a little sketch, and strutting out of the restaurant. When he was really old, with his fame at a peak, he probably could have gone shopping for CDs at Tower with just a pad and some charcoal. A watercolor for a home entertainment center. An oil for a car. A mural for a house. What a guy.

You and I will never be able to do that. What are we going to do, stop in Sizzler, chow down on the salad bar, do a stupid card trick, torture Teller and split? We don't think so. We can't all be Picasso; in fact, only one of us could be Picasso and the position was filled by a Spanish guy.

We do think we should all have the experience of being extraordinarily talented at least once in our life, even though we don't deserve it.

Here's one to try the next time you have dinner with someone you want to impress for sexual, social, or business reasons (maybe all three at once). When you're being led to your seat, stop off, pretending to head to the rest room[1] while the rest of your party sits down. Ask the maître d' who your server is going to be.

Take your waiter or waitress aside and explain that you want to pay your whole check in advance and play a little trick on your friends.

Let the restaurant make an impression of your credit card and then sign the slip. Tell the person in charge that when the meal is over, you'd like a 20 percent tip plus five bucks added to the bill, and you'll trust them to total it. At a 20-percent-plus-five-dollar tip, they won't rip you off, but, just to be sure, check your credit card receipt when it comes at the end of the month. (You should be doing that every month anyway but we'll save further comments like this for *Penn & Teller's Home Financial Tricks*.)

Rehearse with the server a little. Tell him/her that when the meal is

---

[1] If you do every trick in this book at one meal, you'll go to the rest room nine times.

over, you'll be doodling absentmindedly on a napkin or small piece of paper. Tell the server to look over your shoulder at the sketch and say, "Excuse me, our cook and owner are real art fans. Would you mind if I show them this? I think they might love it."

You say "Sure," and shrug at the rest of your party.

The waiter or waitress is to come back, stutter, look really uncomfortable and say, "We'd like to say that if we could keep this, the meal…and the tip are on the house. It's worth so much more, but if you'd be kind enough, we'd really like it." Since a little over 73 percent of waiters and waitresses in major cities are actors, this will be an easy role.

When it happens, you'll feel great. You can scam yourself. You'll feel proud, like a talented artist.

If you tend to take people to one particular restaurant you could even set it up to happen automatically every time you show up. It's hard to have this one make you any money[2]—you pick up the whole check plus five bucks, but it's worth it to feel like Picasso for a moment. To feel like you can coast through life on your enormous talent.

This is the perfect place in the book to make some snotty comment about how "outsider" art is really popular with fancy-assed idiots who couldn't tell your mindless sketches from the stuff they think is worth thousands. But we don't believe that. We dig outsider art. There's some great stuff, and if we owned a restaurant Elliot Freeman and Tony Fitzpatrick could pay every time with sketches…and you…well…AmEx, Master-Card, and Visa are cheerfully accepted.

Don't believe your own hype, Pablo.

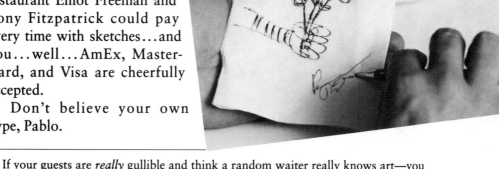

---

[2] If your guests are *really* gullible and think a random waiter really knows art—you could try to sell them your art at home. But even *we* don't think it'll work.

HOW TO BE THE COOLEST PERSON
AT A PICNIC

It's hard to be cool at a picnic. You lug food and try to keep it from spoiling by lugging ice. You lug furniture or blankets or sit in the mud. Then you eat off dishes (which you lug home afterward and try to wash after the remains have ossified) or paperware (which blows over and has to be disposed of in a trash bin five miles away). If the menu is not limited to cold food (which by mealtime is just under body temperature), you must roll a "portable" barbecue up a mountainside with a ten-pound bag of charcoal briquettes on your back. Grilled cheese in the comfort of your kitchen beats *foie gras* in the wilderness any day.

But a picnic does offer you one prop you won't likely have at home. If you've got the nerve, it will make you an instant legend in your community.

The prop? Ants.

The trick? Eat them.

The method? Just do it.[1] Overcome your conditioned aversion to bugs. Ants may be an annoyance in the sleeping bag, but are a nutritious food, enjoyed by people all over the world. In Colombia canned carpenter ants are a popular supermarket item (they can the big juicy ones for people to fry up in butter). NOTE: Avoid ants that bite, and don't eat red fire ants—in large quantities they are toxic.

[1] This is the same method we used on our 1990 TV special to handle a hundred thousand bees without gloves or masks. We took precautions, of course: We had our doctor check to make sure that we were not allergic to bee stings (see the rule of No Permanent Damage, page 86). But there was no trick—we just did it. Teller got only three stings, probably because he poured them by the hatful on Penn. Penn was too busy talking to treat the bees gently, and got stung twenty-four times, including once inside the mouth. His feet swelled up and the skin peeled off his testicles. As far as venom allergies are concerned, Penn has an Achilles' heel and scrotum.

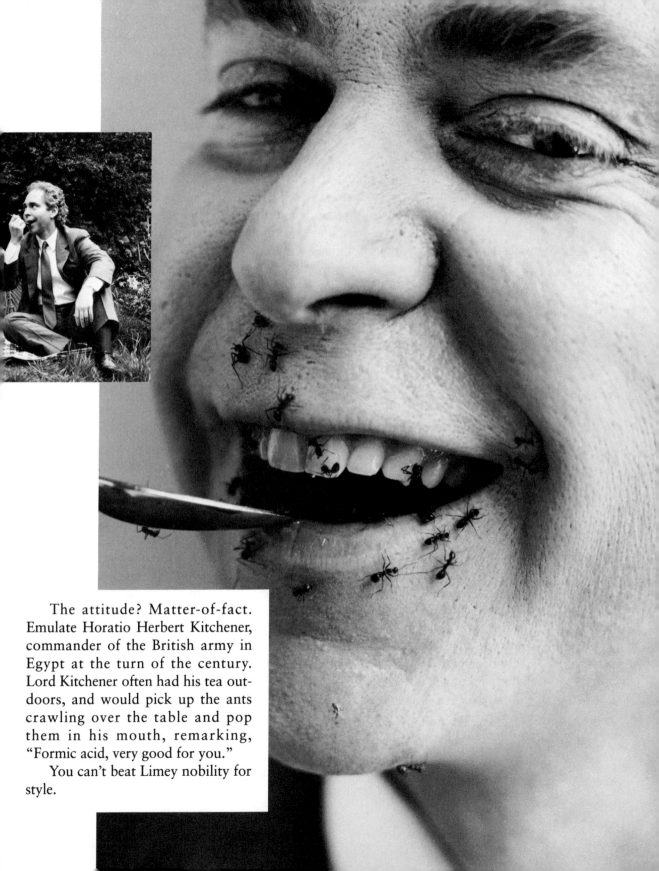

The attitude? Matter-of-fact. Emulate Horatio Herbert Kitchener, commander of the British army in Egypt at the turn of the century. Lord Kitchener often had his tea outdoors, and would pick up the ants crawling over the table and pop them in his mouth, remarking, "Formic acid, very good for you."

You can't beat Limey nobility for style.

THE RIDDLE OF THE SIX DEAD FISH

We sat in our office in a seedy apartment building on Times Square in New York City. It was late afternoon and we had an idea for a television appearance:

We would go on *Late Night with David Letterman.* We would borrow the dapper Mr. Letterman's handsome watch and demolish it on the studio floor with a sledgehammer. Then we'd wheel out a giant aquarium, such as you might see in a fancy seafood restaurant. It would be filled with carp, bass, grouper, and other large fish, gliding majestically through the shimmering water. We would sprinkle the pieces of destroyed watch into the tank, where they would vanish, melting like snowflakes. David would then be asked to choose a fish and scoop it out in a net. He'd dump the fish, still flapping, on a newspaper on his desk. We'd whip out a dagger, slice the fish open, and ask Letterman to reach inside and remove his watch, completely restored, covered in fish entrails.

We loved everything about it: the image of the tank teeming with life; the choosing of the victim by an omnipotent intruder; the ritual disembowelment and epiphany.

And then it hit us. We would have to *kill a fish.* Now, millions of fish are slain every day. They devour each other. Scandinavians harvest them by the ton. But something in our gut told us that if we were to behead and eviscerate a fish on television as part of a magic trick, all hell would break loose. Animal advocates would send NBC a hundred thousand outraged letters. Well, maybe not a hundred thousand—most animal lovers seem less concerned about cold, slimy animals than furry ones with big eyes. But still, a lot. They would rail that the fish was dying not to feed the hungry but as cheap, gladiatorial amusement.

Okay, we reasoned, we could skip dinner, fry up the fish after the trick, and dine right there on camera. Our fish would have both artistic and nutritional value. Viewers would know there was no waste involved. That would head off the complaints.

So we proposed the trick to Robert Morton, the producer of the Letterman show. We respect Morty. His instincts about what will and will not work in comedy are impeccable. "The part with the watch—" he said, "that's great. But killing the fish...? Frankly, I don't think snuff-magic's going to play funny."

He was right, of course. It was the '90s and it was out of fashion to think death was a joke. Even fake death in the movies was getting a bad rap from people too terrified to walk to the corner store. So we suggested an alternative, less dramatic but more digestible.

We would display the fish as food instead of wildlife. We'd bring out a supermarket counter with half a dozen dead fish on shaved ice with price-per-pound signs by each one. Letterman would take his choice, and the watch would appear inside the chosen one.

"Bingo," said Morty.

So that's the way we did it. And on December 19, 1991, when David Letterman pulled his costly chronometer from the guts of a lake trout, everybody laughed.

And not a tear was shed for the six dead fish.

Now and then, as we sit in our office in Times Square, listening to the distant gunshots as the sun goes down, we get to thinking about those fish.

To spare people the pain of seeing one fish die, we killed six (*we* didn't kill them ourselves—we bought them from a fishmonger, but it amounts to the same thing). It was probably the right thing to do, given the circumstances. But it leaves us with a riddle. Why is one fish dying tragic, but six fish dead are funny?

Maybe someday in our theater show, where we're the only ones to face the consequences, we'll try the original, beautiful idea, with the glistening tank full of big fish and the broken watch melting in the water. We'll scoop out the chosen victim, sacrifice it, and resurrect the watch from its entrails.

Then we'll cook it up, cut it in tiny pieces, and divide it among the audience. Maybe we'll do the multiplying bread loaves, too, just to make sure there's enough to feed the multitude.

With the right patter it could be quite an act.

HOW TO TRANSPORT DAVID LETTERMAN'S WATCH INTO THE BELLY OF A FISH

A Professional Food Trick in Twenty-five Easy Steps

1. Find someone who is (a) willing to do anything. This man is Robbie Libbon, our Director of Covert Activities. He is (b) clever. He is (c) devious. He is (d) and (e) good at lying and keeping secrets. He has (f) nerves of steel. Now (b) thru (f) are all wonderful qualities, but would be meaningless without (a). Robbie is the man who (b) built the truck that ran over Teller on our 1990 NBC special and (a) and (f) tested it by lying under the tires and getting run over first.

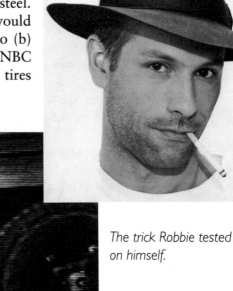

The trick Robbie tested on himself.

2. Now build a box. Actually, since you have found somebody who will do anything, have *him* build a box. It should look like a table at a fishmonger's store, with a sloping top and a lip to keep ice and fish from sliding onto the floor.

3. Hinge the back of the box, and cut a little trapdoor in the upper corner. Open the door and invite your DCA to step inside. If he says, "Sure, that looks like fun," you know you have hired wisely.

4. Test the little trap-door.

5. Get (by now, of course, you understand this means, "Ask your DCA to get") six dead fish and six 6" x 10" pieces of sheet metal. Roll the sheet metal into tubes and seal the seam with duct tape. Every major prop we use is held together with duct tape.

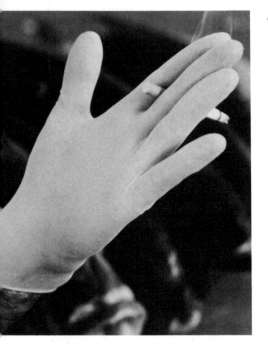

6. Don rubber gloves. THIS IS VERY IMPORTANT. Reeking of dead fish can end friendships; a magic trick can only make or break your career.

7. With a very sharp knife cut a gash in the side of each fish. Impale your fish on your tubes.

8. Cut six holes in the top of your box. Insert a fish-capped tube in each hole. Buy sixty pounds of ice and dump it on the table to hide the tubes (and slow the fish decay).

CARP
.99/lb.

WHITE CARP
1.15/lb.

JACKFISH
1.20/lb.

SNAPPER
2.39/lb.

LAKE TROUT
1.39/lb.

BLUEFISH
1.19/lb.

9. See? It looks like a fish market display. No one suspects that there's a tube running from the guts of each fish, through the ice and into the table...

10. ...where your DCA waits, pelted by a cold, rancid rain of melted ice and fish blood.

11. This is an apt moment to offer your DCA a long contract at plausible wages.

12. If you haven't already done so, get booked on *Late Night with David Letterman.*

13. Find out what brand and model of watch David wears, and find a jeweler who sells it. Tell the jeweler you need a duplicate dummy watch to use in a magic trick—it doesn't have to work, so he can make it out of old parts. He will enjoy the prospect of having his merchandise mauled on national television.

14. On the night of the show, put the duplicate watch in your pocket and wheel the fish-box onto the *Late Night* set. Under ordinary circumstances, you would not consider undergoing the effort of moving

a prop, but you really can't expect your DCA to do it unless he (g) has a twin. Greet Mr. Letterman and borrow his handsome chronometer. As you pass it carelessly from one hand to the other, making him nervous, switch it for your duplicate. Sneak the real one into your left side pocket.

15. Whack the dummy watch on David's desk. Fling it on the studio floor. Dance on it with your cowboy boots. Hit it with a sledgehammer. David will be appalled. He will make brilliantly wry and funny comments, but inwardly he will grieve.

16. Apologize. Offer him a fish in trade. Step up to the fish-box and invite him to choose one. Avoid saying "Name a fish," as that is too easy a setup and you don't want to insult his professional pride.

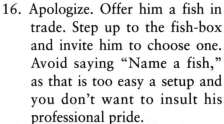

17. Meanwhile, step behind the box, right next to the little trapdoor. Allow your DCA to pick your pocket.

18. When Mr. Letterman announces his selection, your DCA goes to work. He uses the butt end of a screwdriver to ram the watch into the belly of the selected fish.

19. Give your DCA time to get the watch firmly in place and withdraw the tube. Stick the point of a butcher knife into the fish's eye. Remark on how fresh it is. The audience will be too busy controlling their nausea to notice any delays or accidental bumps your DCA gives the fish.

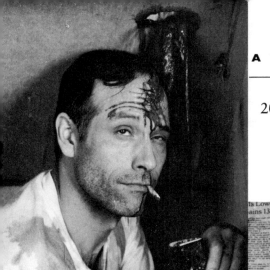

20. Remove the fish from the ice. With the fish and the tube out of the way, iced fish water will be cascading in on your DCA. This is the supreme test of (a).

21. The work is done. Now the fun begins. Slice open the fish. Show the guts. Enjoy.

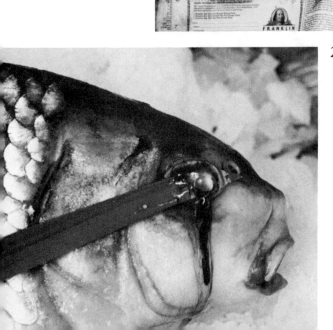

22. Invite Mr. Letterman to reach inside. Watch his love of good timing struggle with his loathing of stinking fish guts.

23. Timing will triumph. He will remove the watch. The fine leather band will be soaked in fish offal.

24. Take a bow. Pick up other dead fish and dance around with them.

25. Remove the fish-box from the set. Take it to a secluded corner and release your DCA. Have him clean everything up.

JESUS OF McDONALD'S

No list of food tricks would be complete without the "Water to Wine Trick." Many have performed it throughout history, but the most famous description is in the bible. It's been said that this particular performance was a real miracle, not a trick. We weren't there, we can't say for sure, but, if there were a god and he wanted to intervene in earthly events, it seems he'd pick something a little harder to duplicate and a tad classier. But what the hell do we know? Apologists say god works in mysterious ways; maybe he hoped the "son of god" would get billing as the "Human Bar-gun."

We are teetotalers. We are anti-drinking and anti-drug. You will never see either one of us in a beer ad or holding a glass of wine. We will not be associated with drugs or alcohol. When Penn did *Miami Vice* he wouldn't let them put a drink in front of him in the bar scene. So we will not teach you the "Water to Wine Trick." If it were up to us, you wouldn't drink alcohol. Of course, it isn't up to us, and it shouldn't be up to us, but we're not going to pose for pictures with wine. It's our goddamn book.

We also don't want to endorse any particular fast-food joints. We eat a lot of fast-food, but this book has no product placement. That being said, this trick works best at McDonald's. You can do it other places but Mickey D's has great straws, really great straws; thick, strong, a good length—you can actually suck a thick shake though them. If you want a good straw, go to the Golden Arches, and we weren't paid to say that.

Here's the deal. When you're ordering, watch what your friend orders for a drink and order a different color: If they order the caramel-colored cola or orange, you order the clear lemon-lime, and vice versa. If they order a shake or coffee, well, you're up the creek without a straw. If you want a cola and they order cola, don't worry, just order the lemon-lime. It doesn't matter what you drink with your burger, it's all just fizzy sugar water anyway. Just order the same size of a contrasting-colored beverage.

Humans naturally divide labor at the fast-food counter. One person grabs the food and the other grabs the drinks. Make sure you're the one who grabs the drinks. Let the mark (see footnote, page 81) go ahead while you linger behind to get napkins and straws.

Unwrap two straws and stick one all the way down to the bottom of each beverage. The liquid in the straw will rise until it's even with the top of the drink. You'll have one straw's worth of beverage in the straw.

Put your finger over the top of each straw. Torricelli's good buddy, atmospheric pressure, will hold the liquid in the straw. Switch them. Now, you have a strawful of caramel color in the clear cup and a strawful of clear in the caramel color (if you're working with orange, do the math in your head). The cool thing is: it won't mix. The foreign sample will keep its integrity for the jostling walk to the table and for a good long while after. For once, the difference in the osmotic pressure is on your side.

From here on in, it's just acting. You can go a couple of ways. You can look at the chump's drink quizzically disgusted and say, "Damn, they got a little cola in your clear beverage, let me see if I can get it out." You reach over, stare at the cup, and wiggle the straw around a little like you're gathering the alien bits of beverage. Once you've "got it," put your finger over the top, pull the straw out, and have your friend watch as you pour it into the ashtray. (McDonald's ashtrays are gold or silver and show beverage color clearly.) If there's no ashtray you can just dump it on the table, but make sure you clean it up before you leave; a high school kid at minimum wage shouldn't have to work harder because you scammed a buddy.

That's one whole presentation. It's neat, quick, easy, and funny and doesn't insult anyone's view of the universe. It just makes the world a little wackier (see page 82). The other presentation is a little meaner. You've already figured it out from the title, it's just a question of how far you want to take it.

Yup, if you're dining at Mick's with christians, you can own them! Get them on the subject of miracles. Smart money says, if you'll listen, they'll talk. You'll have to sit through forcing the blind to see, raising the dead, and the loaf-and-fish bit (see page 116), but eventually they'll get around to the "Water to Wine" gag. If a proselytizer takes a sip of soda before getting to it, don't worry—they'll never notice the difference in taste (it's all just fizzy sugar water), and yours is still set up.

When they mention water to wine, right out of the blue say, "How hard is that?" Say it really innocently.

They'll say something along the lines of "What?"

You say, "How hard is it to turn water into wine? Is that a really hard thing? Making blind people see takes lasers and stuff and moving a big rock takes a lot of people but how hard is it to turn water into wine?"

Whatever they say, you say, "I'd like to give it a try." Look at the drinks and say, "This will do. What is this?" (This is an important step because it reminds them what's in the cup.) They'll tell you.

Put your finger over the straw and pull out a strawful. Repeat what's in the cup, let's say it's cola, "Cola, huh? How hard could it be to change cola to lemon-lime?"

Here you ad-lib like a motherhubbard. You can pray, make magic gestures, forgive everyone at Mickey D's for their trespasses, try your tongue at glossolalia, even swear your life to celibacy (we don't care unless you're attractive and attracted to one of us—in which case just forgive the patrons and forget the celibacy).

Slide your finger off the straw and let the "transformed" liquid spill into the ashtray. Look at it closely for a second, let a smile light up your face, and say, "Wow, I did it. Cool."

Where you go from here is on your head. If you're in the right place at the right time, this might be enough for you to establish your own TV ministry.

And if you can find a victim who drinks wine through a straw, well...

If you bring your lunch from home, here's a way to drive your friends crazy and chisel a niche in the dining hall of fame.

Get a small apple and a big orange. The correct proportions are apple/orange = Teller/Penn. Peel the orange very carefully, keeping as much of the skin as possible undamaged. An excellent way to achieve this is to cut four equally spaced incisions radiating from the "navel" of the orange to points about halfway down the side, then carefully peel down the flaps and pull out the fruit, leaving the other end of the skin intact. You may find it helpful to loosen things up by working a spoon between the skin and the flesh. Now insert the apple into the orange peel and close up the flaps. You will find that the moist inner surface of the peel will want to stick to the apple skin and hold it closed. In an hour or two, the three incisions will shrivel slightly and look like wrinkles in the orange skin. Stick this homemade hybrid in your lunchbox.

When the noon whistle blows, sit down with your friends and start to eat. First finish your sandwich; it's hard to play comedy when you're hungry. Besides, you want your friends to have eaten enough to be willing to look up from their grub to see your trick.

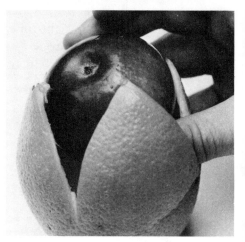

Then take out the orange and start to peel it. Grasp it by the previously opened end, holding the flaps firmly closed. Now use your teeth to nick the peel at the unbroken end; it's uncouth, but commands attention. Then rip at the nick with your fingers and tear off the peel in smallish pieces, making sure your friends glimpse the red apple inside the newly torn orange skin. Incidentally, by the time you finish, you will have destroyed all evi-

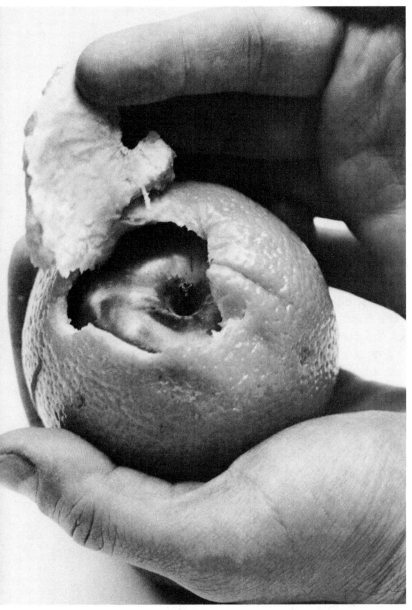

dence of your secret preparation.

Resist any urge to point out what you are doing. Do *not* say, in a voice like Sir Noel Coward's, "Good heaven, what have we here!" Do *not* act awestruck, like a mime discovering a butterfly. Just peel it, eat the apple, and continue the conversation as if nothing is happening. If somebody asks, "Didn't you just take an apple out of that orange peel?" simply reply "No." The flat-out denial of an obvious truth—especially one as silly as the identity of a fruit—is a fine existential joke.

No doubt someone will point to the orange peelings and say, "Then where did *those* come from?" Don't flinch. Look her/him straight in the eye and say, "I don't know." The more convincing and innocent your style, the better the effect. Your friends may realize you are putting them on, but you will still drive them nuts.

Keep up the act, and later if your lunchmates describe what you did, claim they're lying. *Do not crack.* If you own up to doing something as idiotic as sticking an apple into an orange peel, you will be dismissed as a mere prankster. But if you stick to your story, people will not know what to think. Did anything *really* happen? Are you crazy? Are they?

And you will live in lunchroom legend.

HOW TO USE THAT STUPID
LITTLE SUGAR PACKET

This book comes with a sugar packet. Take a look at it. It's the thing in the Gimmicks envelope that looks like a sugar packet. Got it? Try to rip it open. You can't. It's made out of Kevlar-or-something. It can't be ripped, but it looks like a regular sugar packet.

This is a gag that you want to have on you at all times. Put the sugar packet in your pocket[1] or bag right now, and keep it there. Try to keep it clean but don't worry about it getting torn and spilling, it's Kevlar-or-something for christ's sake and you can't tear it. That's the point.

You can't really plan when to do this trick; you have to wait for the right situation to arise. Wait until you're out eating and someone who uses sugar orders coffee or tea. When that happens, get our fake sugar packet in the front of the sugar and Sweet'n Low holder. There isn't really a move for this, you just have to do it. Maybe you'll get lucky and the chump will turn around or get up and go to the bathroom and you can make your move. If that doesn't happen, reach into the sugar holder, take out a packet and leave the fake one behind. It's really not very hard. You can practice it a couple times when you're eating alone and have nothing better to do.

Once you've got the sugar packet in the front, you hope[2] they take the front sugar packet. Most people do. If they don't, keep hoping; they

---

[1] If you have a left breast pocket, you might want to carry our fake sugar packet there. It's made of Kevlar-or-something. That's the stuff used in bulletproof vests.

If you happen to be an innocent victim of a drive-by shooting, and they happen to shoot you right in the heart and the lead pill happens to hit the fake sugar packet in your breast pocket, and you live and tell the press that you got the fake sugar packet from Penn & Teller, it sure as hell isn't going to hurt our book sales.

We'll go a step further: If you take a bullet in the chest and tell the press that the Penn & Teller fake sugar packet saved your life, give us a call and we'll give you another fake sugar packet free and you can keep the old one as a souvenir.

Keep in mind that with the small surface area of the fake sugar packet to distribute the force of a bullet, more likely than not you'll have a cheesy fake sugar packet wrapped around a bullet going through your heart at just under the speed of sound instead of just the bullet. Your P&T souvenir will be buried inside your chest.

But if it does happen to save your life, try to mention Penn & Teller.
Thanks.

[2] If you forget to hope, don't worry. The best thing about hoping and praying is that they don't work. You can even hope against hope that they don't take the sugar packet you want them to take and the outcome will be the same. Cool, huh?

may use it for a refill. If the meal ends without them taking the bait, just put it back in your pocket and try again later. (Better yet, leave it there to work its mischief without you and buy another copy of our book just to get another stupid, fake sugar packet.)

When the mark (see footnote, page 81) has taken the ersatz sugar packet, the fun work starts. You'll want to play your fish like a fish (see pages 116–27). When they start to try to rip, you start talking. Talk about anything, but talk earnestly. Talk about your aunt's stomach operation. Make the fish be polite and keep him/her looking in your eyes while struggling to open the packet. It'll make them crazier if you don't let them look down. You'll find that the longer they're trying to rip the packet the less they'll really be listening to you. You can start saying stuff like "…and then my aunt turned into a CD player and flew around under her own power…" This is the fun part; enjoy it. As you keep their eyes on your eyes, watch their mind freaking over our stupid sugar packet.

Eventually, the next step will happen. They will put down the fake sugar packet and pick up another. Keep talking to them—stop them from thinking. What happens next may be the most beautiful thing you'll ever see. You will watch your patsy use all their strength to rip apart a normal, defenseless sugar packet. It's gorgeous. Sugar flies everywhere. It'll hit people at the next table. It'll be the high point of your life. Work fast at this instant and you can be sure they'll go crazy. While they're apologizing to others in the restaurant for throwing sugar at them, while they're flustered and confused, while chaos is ruling—pick up our phony sugar packet and put it back in your pocket or bag. Isn't that pretty?[3]

After you've gotten rid of the evidence, ask the loser what the hell is wrong. They'll explain that they couldn't rip the sugar packet. They'll start looking for the untearable packet. They won't find it unless they frisk you. They'll just rip every sugar packet on the table and think they're crazy. It's moments like this that make life worth living.

You've had your fun. You have the packet back on your person and you're ready to do it again, the next time fortune smiles.

---

[3] Magicians' jargon for "well choreographed."

Here's a different kind of holiday food fun, a story for kids. We've written it so that any youngsters grade four or higher can read it for themselves. It's a seasonal story, all about the spirit of Hallowe'en. Give it to a kid to read alone, then ask the young reader to tell you about the story. It's a fun way to reinforce the themes about holiday safety.

THE STORY OF LITTLE GINNY GOBLIN AND THE DANCING KANDY KORN

A *Really Spooky* Story You Can Read All by Yourself

IT WAS THE NIGHT BEFORE Hallowe'en and little Ginny Goblin was getting her costume ready for her favorite night of the year. All through the summer she had been planning her costume, and now old Granny Greta Goblin was putting the finishing touches on it. Ginny was going this year as a Ghoul, and Granny Greta had made her a gorgeous green *crêpe de chine* aura, and shiny embroidered drops of red silk blood dripping from stuffed white flannel fangs. Oh, how pretty Ginny was!

Being a goblin child was hard work. Every day Ginny went to Spirit School, where she had morning classes in Mischief and Affliction, then after lunch Love-Frustration, Premature-Aging, and Rumor-Mongering.

But in the Spirit World, Hallowe'en was a high holiday, and school recessed for a whole week before and after to allow the Sprites and Spritettes to celebrate. All Ginny's ghostly relatives from around the world were coming for a family reunion. When Ginny thought about seeing her second cousin, Gary Gremlin, she blushed a pale green. She had always had a secret crush on Gary, with his pert horns and his cute pointy tail. All right, by now the adults have been convinced that this is nauseating children's junk that you can read for yourself. They've handed the book over to you. They're watching the evening news. *Say nothing.* Just sit there with an angelic smile on your unwrinkled little face, and pretend you're thrilled with a harmless fantasy-romance. Pay careful attention.

Hallowe'en is a holiday that grown-ups love. It's a chance to trick kids into dressing up in dopey costumes. Why? So that the adults can take pictures. Then, just about the age the kid starts dating, the adults "re-discover" these embarrassing monstrosities. And the instant a prospective boyfriend or girlfriend steps in the door, out come the snapshots with cries of "I just *had* to show you how cute Jesse looked twelve years ago dressed as a squirrel." You think we're exaggerating? Ignore the bogus caption on the following pictures and see for yourself. The kid on the left is Teller, convinced he's Merlin, in bad beard and pointy hat. The one on the right is Penn in a Pumpkin suit.

"…Everywhere ran happy children,
beautifully dressed, laughing and sharing their treats…"

Now do you believe us? That's why we're going to teach you a way to protect yourself.

On the afternoon of Hallowe'en go into the kitchen. Pour a tablespoon of pancake syrup into a paper cup. Add a few drops of red food coloring to the syrup, enough to make it look like blood fresh from a gash. Then clean up the evidence. Take the cup of "blood" and hide it somewhere you can get to it quickly and easily when you come home from trick-or-treating. Finally, get an apple and hide it in your room. You're all set. That evening, put on your costume and slip the apple in your trick-or-treat bag. As you leave the house, your family will stop you. They will take pictures. (*Now* do you believe us?)

When you return, plunk your bag of goodies on the table. Say, "Boy, that was fun. We even stopped in on that crazy lady who lives in the basement around the corner—you know, the one you told us never to talk to. There was a whole bunch of us, though, so it was okay to go into her house. But what a lousy treat! She must be some kind of health nut. All she had was apples." While your folks bawl you out for disobeying them, step casually over to your hidden cup of blood, and suck up a *small* mouthful. (You don't need too much, as it will mix with saliva and seem like gallons, and you don't want to start gagging early.) Then walk straight over to the bag of treats. Reach in, pull out the apple you put there, and bite into it. Scream. Let red pancake syrup and saliva drip out of your mouth. Claw at your face and make strangling noises.

Your family will instantly remember Hallowe'en horror stories and assume that their precious darling has bitten into an apple some maniac has spiked with razor blades. They will panic and cry and, if your acting is good enough, maybe faint.

This works even better as a team effort by an older and a younger sibling. The younger one loads up with the "blood" outside the house, and the older one tells the story. Then Junior shrieks his guts out right on the word "apples." Also, consider making the villain in the story a specific neighbor you know the grown-ups hate. That makes the whole show more believable and terrifying.

If you do this trick well, they may punish you. That's life. But as you're sitting alone in your room, don't think about the cartoons you're missing. Enjoy the sweetness of revenge taken in advance. Remember that someday they would have smugly shown those snapshots to your friends, and laughed. But now the same pictures will bring only memories of horror. So your dignity is safe.

One final note: *Don't tell them where you learned this trick.* If you say, "I got it from the Penn & Teller book," they'll take the book away and never let

you read it again, and it's full of great
tricks you're *really* going to love doing.
Instead blame the bully who kicks you
in gym class. Tell them, "He said he
wanted to show me a joke that would
make my whole family happy. He's
such a liar." Be careful you don't get
caught; if they decide to complain to the
bully's parents, stop them with "Why warn
them? They deserve to suffer—they made
him the rat he is."

All clear? Good. Now, go thank your
parents for letting you read the cute
Hallowe'en story. In case they quiz you on the
plot, here's a quick summary: Little Ginny
Goblin's cousin Gary Gremlin hated Hallowe'en
and was reckless about the
rules of Hallowe'en safety. He
took candy from strangers,
crossed the street on red lights, and was run
over by a pumpkin truck. So Ginny made a
magic bonfire and all the children poured their
treats onto it. Suddenly the Kandy Korn started to
dance (you have to get the title in somehow) and
marched right down Gary's throat, which made him
come back to life.

In case your resident adult scans the last para-
graphs of the story for redeeming social value—here's a
few dummy closing sentences in the insipid style they
expect:

Ginny took Gary's hand. "See? We loved you all the

time, even when you were mean and spiteful. Love brought you back to life."

In a soft voice Gary replied, choking back tears, "I will always remember this night, and whenever I feel selfish or reckless or inclined to play cruel tricks, I will remember the magic of the Dancing Kandy Korn."

Gary stayed true to his word. He grew up strong and handsome, and excelled equally at sports, academics, and stock market forecasting. When he reached the age to marry, he asked—guess who? Ginny!—who accepted, and together they served their community's recycling and reforestation programs, and lived...

happily ever after.

THE VANISHING APPETIZER

SETTING: A restaurant.

PROBLEM: The server has just delivered the appetizers. Your companion's appetizer looks better than yours.

OBJECTIVE: Eat your companion's appetizer without him/her knowing how you did it.

METHOD

Your friend is just about to dig in when you say, "Do you find yourself eating too fast and barely taking time to enjoy your food?" This question should put the brakes on, at least enough to let you get out the

◀ *Theirs.*

next line. "Well, then, you might be interested in a visualization[1] technique that will not only help you slow down, but will enhance your experience of your food's flavor."

How can your friend resist? You're offering something to make eating—already a nearly perfect activity—even better.

So you continue, "Here's what you do. First, take a minute to look intensely at what you're about to eat. Study it. Appreciate it as you would a work of art. Memorize every shape, color, and smell on the plate." Your friend looks, sniffs, and starts to salivate.

"Now relax," you say, reaching across the table with both hands,

Yours. ◗

---

[1] We're talking about the type of training in which people pay money to learn how to imagine they have attained their goals; the notion is that all you have to do to get rich is picture yourself in a limousine, and the rest will happen automatically. It's a featured item on the curriculum of the something-for-nothing school of self-help.

and lightly massaging your companion's temples. "Relax," you repeat as if trying to induce a trance. Meanwhile, move your hands inward from the temples, and stroke the forehead above the eyebrows with your index fingers.

Say, "Now let your eyes close, but continue to picture your food. Try to see it in color with all the shapes and textures." Continue to stroke the forehead, but the instant your friend's eyes are closed, extend your right little finger. Then, on the next stroke, quickly pull your left hand out of the way, and rest your right index finger lightly

on your friend's right eyelid and your right little finger on his/her left eyelid. Your friend will think you have the index finger of each hand on an eyelid, and will have no idea that one of your hands is free. Quietly snatch the *hors d'oeuvre* off his/her plate.

Continue in a soft, hypnotic voice, "Now imagine you are eating your appetizer. As you picture each step, tell me about it. Describe all the nuances and details." As your companion describes the imaginary delicacy, you eat the real one. You will find your ill-gotten gourmandizing piquantly satisfying.

When you are finished, bring your left hand up near your friend's face as you say, "Now, when I count to three, open your eyes. One..." Lift your fingertips from your friend's eyelids. Immediately switch positions so that your right index finger is touching your friend's left cheek, just under the eye, and your left index finger is touching your friend's right cheek in a symmetrical position. Count, "...two...three!" Your friend opens his/her eyes and sees you remove your two index fingers, just as though they had been in use all the time. By the way, make sure you remember to fold in that telltale right little finger.

Look at your friend with great intensity (trying to keep your friend from looking down at the food) and ask, "So what do you think? Would you order it again?"

When your friend answers, say wistfully, "Hm. Sounds delicious. *Mine* was a little dry." Immediately change the subject. Talk rapidly and excitedly about some event in the news. Make it hard to interrupt you.

If you act your part well, your friend will be totally confused. And if she/he manages to slip in "What happened to my food?" look puzzled and say, "You ate it, of course. You were just raving about how good it was, and how you would order it again!"

Don't worry about getting caught on this one. Once you've scarfed the snack, the game is over, though there is still lots of fun to be had by insisting your friend ate the appetizer herself/himself. As a matter of fact, it's even more fun when he/she is *sure* you're the culprit, but just doesn't know how you did it. So don't hesitate to leave a little spinach between your teeth (see page ix).

By the way, if there are other people at the table seeing how the trick is done, don't let them cramp your style. Take them into your confidence, and watch how they back up your story about who ate what.

CORNSTARCH—A LITTLE LESSON IN LIFE

Quick, don't ask questions, just take a box of cornstarch, put it in a bowl, add a cup and a half of water and play with it. Add some more water. Play with it some more. We don't care how cool you think you are, just do it. You're not setting up a trick, you're playing. It's cheap, easy and waiting for you in your kitchen. Oh, if only dating could be like cornstarch.

Are you having fun? You'll notice right away that your mixture is viscoelastic. The cornstarch forms really long-chain molecules. When the gunk is diluted or deformed gently and slowly, these honking chains can rearrange themselves and stay liquid. But, when there's enough of these molecules crammed together and the impact is fast and hard enough, they don't have the time or room to rearrange their big old selves. They stay all tangled, and the viscosity becomes enormous. With violence all around it, the slime cops to a solid. Like a lot of us, its viscosity is dependent on stress. Non-Newtonian city.

What this means is, if you have the right amount of water (and it's not hard to get the right amount of water, just do it), it looks like milk. If you put your fist against it, your fist sinks into the gooey mess, but if you punch it hard, your fist bounces off. Counterintuitive minus zero no limit. If you punch this household magic goo hard enough, you can even get cracks to appear. Awesome.

There are all sorts of tricks to do with this mess. If you swirl it around, in front of someone, it looks kind of like a bowl of milk; it's a fluid you can swirl around gently. Now move it fast, like you're going to throw it at the sucker, and it turns solid from the fast movement and stays in the bowl like rubber. (If you don't have the right density, it will fly out. That's why you point it at someone else.)

If you pick up a handful and keep treating it cruel you can get it to form a solid ball. If you set that cornball down or toss it to someone, like a lot of us, it'll turn mushy and sloppy as soon as it's treated gently. Playing with cornstarch and water can teach you a little science... and maybe a little bit about life.[1]

---

[1] If *Reader's Digest* does a condensed version of this book, that last paragraph is a shoo-in.

SPOON-BREAKING

Misdirection: The Little Lie That Proves the Big One

Elsewhere in this book (page 76) we've called Spoon-Bending a really lousy trick and this a really fine one. Well, it is. But not—pointless atomic whizzing of the universe knows—merely because it does more damage to flatware.

What makes us like Spoon-Breaking is how much you can learn from it about Misdirection, the big secret behind all good magic tricks. Misdirection (see footnote 1, page 66) is a devilishly misleading piece of jargon—just looking at the word you'd probably assume it means distraction, i.e., knocking over the scenery stage right to distract the audience's attention while the famous Vanishing Duck gets yanked off behind a curtain stage left. But real Misdirection is much more cunning.

Think of it this way.

When you see a magician float someone in midair, and you think, "It's got to be wires too thin to see from the auditorium, or a forklift behind the scenery," your common sense is telling you the plain truth. To fool you into thinking someone's floating *without* wires or forklifts, the magician must do something to jam up your common sense and make you believe that the simple, logical explanation is impossible. This "something" is called Misdirection. In a levitation, for example, the magician might pass a hoop around the floatee. Suddenly you find yourself thinking, "Dang! If they can pass a hoop around her/him, then they *can't* be using hard-to-see wires or forklifts behind the backdrop."

Misdirection is the little lie (the hoop) **that gives the audience "proof" of a bigger lie** (that someone is floating without normal support).

So far so good. But now the tough question. Why in the world would you, the audience, *trust* that genuine chrome-plated Make-Your-Levitation-Look-Impossible hoop (the Misdirection), and *doubt* the hard-to-see wires (a reasonable hypothesis based on a lifetime's experience of physics)?

We offer a guess: You trust the hoop because it's more fun. It lets you believe there's a niftier way to float than wires and machinery. It lets you imagine the magician is not just a nerd who sits up nights figuring out how to gimmick hoops, but instead is a scientific or psychological wiz.

So to be really complete in our definition, we ought to say, **Misdirection is the little lie that gives the spectators "proof" of a bigger lie they want to believe.**

THE TRICK

If you want to get a gut feeling for how Misdirection works, you need to learn a trick where everything hinges on it. That's why we're teaching you Spoon-Breaking. In this stunt Misdirection, the Little Lie, convinces people that a prepared spoon is unprepared, allowing them to fall (temporarily—this is just cheap theater[1]) for the emotionally appealing Big Lie: that a person can have mental power so strong it can melt solid metal objects.[2]

But before you can get to any of the exciting Misdirection, you need to start with some secret preparation. This happens long before anybody even suspects you're going to do a trick:

1. Obtain a spoon that matches exactly the spoons that will be available where you're going to perform. This is easy for low-down "psychic" crooks; they just steal one from their host's dishwasher when nobody's looking. In a restaurant they let their host lead the way, and filch a spoon off a neighboring place setting on the way to the table. In a more formal situation, for example, performing for a party in an hotel, they go to the coffee shop for a muffin, and come back with spoons in their pockets. You, being an upright citizen,

---

[1] In entertainment the effect of Misdirection is temporary and harmless; "willing suspension of disbelief" is how Coleridge put it. Somewhere in the back of your mind, you *know* the truth. But in other forms of deception, Misdirection can be used to peddle destructive lies. In Trance Channeling a personal fact about the client—a fact that the channeler "couldn't possibly have known" ("When you were a child you would not eat...just a moment...it's getting clear now...yes, *anchovies*!")—might serve as "proof" that an entity is truly speaking from beyond. In evangelism, "miraculous" healings (see pages 194–95 for Rolly's discussion of the TV preacher, and read James Randi's excellent exposé, *The Faith Healers* [see page 80]) are looked on as "proof" that the healer is in touch with the supernatural. In politics, dubious history ("Reading pornography turned nice-guy Ted Bundy into a psychotic serial killer") is sometimes used to "prove" a general "truth" ("Sexy entertainment makes people do bad things, and therefore we should support censorship"). So it pays to beware when somebody justifies an extraordinary claim with a Hoop.

[2] The very word *power* has sold everything from toy pyramids to seminars in self-control. Wouldn't you rather Increase Your Word Power than enlarge your vocabulary? Don't you prefer to hear the traffic report on your local "Power Radio Station"? When you hear the term "Crystal Power," don't you feel an itch to don quartz on a rope?

will have to find a way to obtain the appropriate matching spoon without violating your own ethics.

2. Get some time alone with your contraband spoon. A stall in a restroom is a good spot for the rendezvous. Muster all your finger strength and bend the thin part where the bowl joins the handle. Bend it back and forth again and again. And again and again and again. Your hands will get really tired and the metal will get hot from all those disgruntled molecules shearing against each other. This may be the most physically strenuous trick-homework you'll have to do in your life.

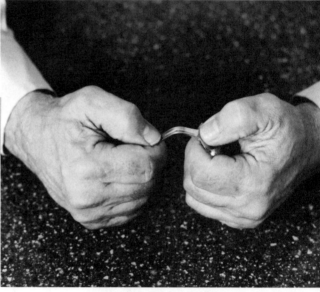

TIP: The cheaper the spoon the easier this is to do.

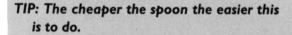

After you have bent it back and forth for a few minutes—don't get impatient—you will detect it getting easier and easier. Slow down. Bend it more gingerly now, until you start to feel that if you held it by the handle, the bowl would *almost*, but not quite, droop. If you look at the handle, you will see a "stress fracture," a tiny break line across the handle. Because you have just stood in a restroom stall for ten minutes making that fracture, it will be incredibly obvious to you. To an untrained eye, misdirected as in the next step, it will be invisible.

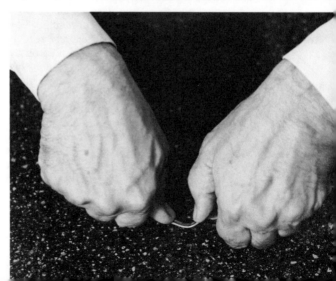

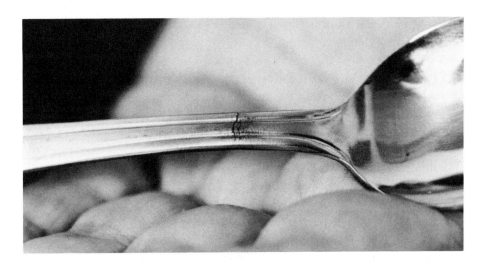

TIP: Don't be discouraged. Your first or second try, you may go too far and break the spoon before you intend to, or end up with a spoon that looks like a cross section of the Alps. Keep trying and you will get it.

3. Now begins the fun part, the Little Lie, the Misdirection. The obvious—indeed the only—possible method for the Spoon-Breaking trick is to prepare the spoon as you did in step #2. *You must now totally rule out that possibility for your audience.* The first step is to get your fractured spoon somewhere your audience thinks you couldn't have planted it. We'll suggest a few strategies:

(a) **At Your Friend's Home:** Once you have a prepared spoon that matches your friend's teaspoons, you might excuse yourself to make a phone call and step into the kitchen. Call your answering machine and meanwhile slip the stressed spoon into your friend's tableware drawer, second or third from the top in the spoon slot (just in case someone needs a spoon before you get around to your trick).

(b) **At a Restaurant:** Watch and wait for the moment your friend looks away or leaves the table, and switch the prepared spoon for one at a nearby unoccupied place setting.[3] Or try performing "The Vanishing Appetizer" and take advantage of the time your friend's eyes are closed to make the switch. Good magicians are opportunists. If all else fails, follow the example of the famous "psychic" who covered a move by spilling a cup of boiling coffee on his observer.

(c) **At a Party in an Hotel:** If you are doing this as a stunt for a large group of people, you can get away with dramatizing the "test conditions" a bit more. So approach some honcho in the group you are performing for. Ask him/her to get you a handful of spoons from the coffee shop. When the bossperson brings back the spoons and puts them down, find an excuse to make her/him turn away for an instant. Let's say you spot a pile of napkins on a nearby table. Point to them and ask the VIP to get one. When he/she turns to get it, *silently* add your spoon to the ones on the table. Put the spoons on the napkin, then have the bigwig fold them inside and stash the bundle in her/his pocket or purse "for security."

4. Let some time pass, then bring the conversation around to the subject of infamous "psychic" stunts and offer to show the Spoon-Breaking Trick. Now comes the most important (and fun) part of the Misdirection, and this is where your acting must be totally believable.

(a) **At Your Friend's Home:** *Remember, you've planted the fractured spoon among your host's utensils in the kitchen drawer.* Have your host bring you a few clean teaspoons from the kitchen. Now ask a question or two to reinforce the idea that you have never seen these spoons before. *Don't* be blatant and say, "Have I ever seen these spoons before?" Make your point subtly by asking a casual question like, "Are these stainless steel?" Then pick up your prepared spoon (as if you couldn't care less which one you were picking up), and, holding it by the end of the handle, tap the bowl of the spoon lightly on the table—just a light tap once or twice (don't break it yet!) as if getting a feel for it. Say, "This will do just fine." Try looking at the underside, as if curious about the manufacturer's name.

---

[3] This ploy is next to impossible to use on somebody with whom you play the Parsley Game (see page 40).

Nod approvingly, and say, "Good quality. Made in Bolivia, doncha know." If you enjoy being really brazen, casually pinch your fingers around the handle to conceal the fracture and hold the spoon right under somebody else's nose to read the maker's mark.

(b) **At a Restaurant:** *You've switched in a spoon in the vacant place setting at the adjacent table.* Look around as though you are afraid of getting caught by the waiter, then snatch the prepared spoon off the place setting with a naughty smile and the remark, "Hell, they'll never notice." Then continue by tapping and examining the spoon as described in (a).

(c) **At the Hotel Party:** *You've arranged to have the honcho ready with the napkin full of spoons.* Call the bigwig who's carrying the spoons to the stage and ask him/her a few carefully worded questions:

YOU: Before the show I asked you to find some spoons and wrap them up in a napkin for me. Did you?

WIG: Yes, I did.

YOU: Where did you get them?

WIG: I went down to the coffee shop and asked to borrow them.

YOU: And where has your bundle of coffee-shop spoons been throughout the show?

WIG: Right here in my pocket.

The way you word your questions allows the muckety-muck to answer truthfully, *and yet the audience is left with the impression that you came nowhere near the spoons!* The selective questioning of a truthful witness in such a way as to imply something false is one of the subtlest ploys of bogus miracle workers.

5. From here on in, it's all theatrics. Have someone hold the ends of the rigged spoon. Rub the fracture point with your index finger and thumb, and push the break line up and down in ever-increasing strokes to weaken the joint more and more. Half-close your eyes as if going into a trance and sing something. Yes, sing. Anything. "America the Beautiful," "Puff the Magic Dragon," "God's Comic," "Fever," "Mandatory Suicide," "Begin the Beguine," "Me So Horny." Anything you sing here will be strangely amusing, and as it becomes more and more apparent that the spoon seems to be "softening" and finally breaking into two, people will be splendidly and totally amazed.

That's it. Spoon-Breaking A to Z. It's a fine trick, but even if you choose not to do this trick, hang on to the principle of Misdirection—the Little Lie that "proves" the seductive big one.

And remember: When something seems too good to be true, it probably is.

HOW ABOUT THOSE OFFICIAL-LOOKING STICKERS IN THE ENVELOPE?

How About a Really Subtle Trick with No Punch Line?

Should the government be forcing nutritional information on our food products? Do we want tax dollars to pay for a bureaucrat to decide where the amount of riboflavin should be printed on a bag of tortilla chips? How much are you willing to pay some committee to mandate the average serving size of wheat crackers? Does anyone *even look* at the nutritional information? Do those that do *really know* what it means? Isn't this stuff supposed to be done for *free* by the invisible free market hand? Will people make healthier choices because of mandatory labeling? What do we know? Dammit Jim,[1] we're magicians, not doctors.

Is it good for practical jokers that our government is meddling in food packaging? Yes, yes, triple yes and a little yahoo. The regulated uniformity has made it possible for people *like us* to print up fake information on stickers and for people *like you* to stick them over the real information. The packaging is standard enough that you should be able to find a sticker in our little Gimmicks envelope that will fit well enough on most any package.

In the first paragraph we implied that not many people even look at the nutritional information, let alone know what it really means, and now we tell you to alter it for a joke…yeah, so? Like we said in the subtitle, it's a subtle joke that probably won't be noticed without you pointing it out, and then you'll have to explain it. Maybe not, but if you happen to know a health-nut chemist who reads all the nutritional information and knows and cares what it all means—these stickers are worth the price of the book several times over.

I don't think we have to tell you how to use the ones at the right. "NO CATTLE WERE HARMED IN ANY WAY DURING THE TESTING AND/OR MANUFACTURE OF THIS PRODUCT" (put this one on a nice juicy steak; also see page 50), the *U* in a circle means kosher, it's great for bacon (see page 53), "CONTAINS 5% LOAM AND OTHER RICH TOPSOIL" (this one is good for carob),

---

[1] James Tiberius Kirk.

CONTAINS NO SUGAR is dedicated to Penn's dad, who's a diabetic. CARRAGEENAN, GUAR GUM, XANTHAN GUM, and AGAR, which are all real ingredients but they're funny words and we all love funny words.

Also on the ingredients list we've got "CONTAINS ALL-NATURAL RICIN." Ricin is a deadly poison. It was injected in pellet form by the "Bulgarian brolly[2]". We have our good friend ETHYLENE GLYCOL, which is antifreeze, but kind of looks like propylene glycol, which is an emulsifier. If one of your friends gets either one of these jokes, sign him or her up as your Morbid Trivial Pursuit partner.

Now that yogurt likes to brag about which living culture they have, we have a sticker that includes "WHOLE BACTERIA CULTURE (MYCOBACTERIUM LEPRAE)." It's leprosy.

Don't be confused by the "HOMEOPATHIC HOLISTIC HEALING POWDER." That sticker is for the trick on page 161, but it wouldn't hurt to stick it on some sea salt.

Have fun. Mix them! Match them! Collect them all!

CONTAINS: CARRAGEENAN, GUAR GUM, XANTHAN GUM, AGAR

CONTAINS ALL-NATURAL RICIN

CONTAINS: ETHYLENE GLYCOL, 46,359 GRAMS OF FAT

HOMEOPATHIC HOLISTIC HEALING POWDER

HIGH FAT LOW FIBER

WARNING: Contents May Be Converted to Pure Energy Equivalent to the Speed of Light Squared Times Its Mass.

ALSO MAKES AN EXCELLENT ALL-NATURAL INSECT REPELLENT

If product touches mucous membranes, wash for three minutes with cold water and call physician.

CONTENTS MAY HAVE SETTLED DURING SHIPPING, RENDERING THEM INEDIBLE.

Serving suggestion: Serve cold with lard.

NUTRITIONAL INFORMATION

Per serving. Aside from the packaging, which contains paper and ink products, this product contains no nutritional value whatsoever.

---

[2] British slang for umbrella/assassination weapon used by bad guys.

THE INCREDIBLY DANGEROUS
GLOWING PICKLE MACHINE

When a regular old dill pickle is skewered on two metal pins and 110 ac, regular old U.S. of A. house current, is run through the pins, the pickle glows a ghostly yellow. It's the most beautifully goofy science thing you'll ever see. Jeffrey Appling at Clemson University has written a paper called "Sodium D Line Emission from Pickles" (he deserves tenure on the title alone) about this phenomenon. He figures sodium ions pick up the electrons and become excited atoms. The yellow sodium D line glow indicates the free atomic emission of sodium. Sounds right to us. We don't really know where the idea for plugging in a pickle started—probably with Martin Gardner (see footnote, page 172). Many cool things start with Martin Gardner.

A few years ago, Penn was on the Alex Bennett radio show in San Francisco. He got much too excited about the glowing pickle. We had done it the day before at Alex's house and we couldn't stop laughing about it on the air. It's a glowing pickle! It's a pickle that lights up, an intrinsically funny thing. We talked about it so much on the air that an Alex Bennett fan whose name we forget (sorry) gave us a great rig for easily lighting pickles. Penn has it mounted on the wall.

When someone visits Penn for the first time, Penn turns out the lights and fires up a pickle. For a good long while (like fifteen seconds), nothing happens. Nothing. Nothing is always funny; you've got people standing in the dark, looking at a pickle impaled on the wall doing nothing. Then, with a sputter, it bursts to life. You couldn't read by it, but you sure can see by it. Wow. It's our favorite thing.

It is also *the* best way to get your favorite attractive person up to your place. If you're sexually turned on by a person who says "no" to coming up and seeing your pickle glow, forget him or her; you can do better. Don't ask him/her out again. But if he/she does come up, you've got this attractive person, laughing him- or herself sick, at your side, by the warm glow of your pickle, in your home. If you can't segue from there into something romantic you need a lot more than a sodium D line emission from your pickle to save your love life.

The glowing pickle has been shown on *The Tonight Show* by Mr. Wizard and it's been written up in *Omni*, but everyone's really afraid of it. Our publisher didn't even want it in the book—"What if someone tries to build it and gets electrocuted?"

We don't want anyone to get hurt but, jesus-goddamn-it-to-hell, does that mean we can't tell people cool things because one fool might misunderstand and get hurt? What is the morality here? What is the legality here? Can we be sued by some nut who grabbed bare electrical wires while reading our book? Would that be our fault? Are we going to be forced by our legal system to write to the lowest common denominator? Do we *have* to write for the idiots? Will these questions seem ironic when read aloud at our trial?

Omni was so careful they wouldn't even print a picture of the thing working, like the one on page 102.

And *Omni* is supposed to be for smart people (although you couldn't tell it from the paranormal garbage they've been known to publish).

So here's the deal: If you know a lot about electricity, you should be able to make a pickle machine with just what we've told you so far. You really don't have to know very much about pickles. All you have to do is run house current through one. Do it safely. Don't touch anything while it's plugged in. Put a fuse on it. Wear a condom.

If you don't know everything about electricity—

DON'T TRY IT!

If you have any question about how much you know about electricity—

DON'T DO IT!

IMPORTANT: No matter how much you know about electricity, before you start working on your pickle machine, handwrite a little note like this ▶

Put your signature on the note, date it, and **Throw this book away!**

> To whom it may concern:
> I got the idea to try to build a glowing pickle machine by watching Mr. Wizard on The Tonight Show Starring Johnny Carson with Jay Leno on January 24, 1990, and reading about it in Scot Morris's Games column in Omni Magazine, December 1990.
> Sincerely:

GETTING CREAMED IN THE MIDDLE OF THE NIGHT AT DENNY'S[1]

There's No Business Like Show Business

Perhaps the saddest truth of showbiz is that for every show person found larger-than-life, debauched, and dead in the Chateau Marmont, there's a multitude of entertainers living their lives in assorted Denny's. Penn & Teller have been on Broadway, in movies, and on TV, and we've spent more time trying to get parsley on each other's plate (see page 40) without getting caught than we've spent nude in Jacuzzis[2] with underaged people of various sexes. This surprises no one. The shocking thing is that the same is true for most entertainers.

Michael Goudeau juggles and tells jokes in Lance Burton's magic show in Vegas. Every night Michael is surrounded onstage and backstage by topless women, glitz, and glamour. I asked him if he knew any food tricks. He lit up.

"There's the 'Creamer Game,'" he said proudly.

I told him we knew Mac King's creamer-in-the-eye gag (see page 3). He said this one wasn't a prank, but a game of skill.

It goes like this:

Contestant A holds a fork in front of his or her chest with the tines out. Contestant B adjusts Contestant A's fork to the desired angle. Contestant B throws the creamer (in the aerodynamically inferior paper-top-leading position) at the fork. If the flying creamer is pierced on the stationary fork, it explodes all over Contestant A. Contestant B is the winner. If it doesn't explode, they switch roles, Contestant B holds the fork and A throws. The game continues until one player "gets creamed" and the other is victorious.

DAVENPORT'S MAPLE FARM & REST.
SHELBURNE, MA   15 MARCH '92

---

[1] Denny's is a brand name. Please see the footnote on page 82.

[2] Ibid.

House of Breakfast
Minneapolis, Mn
July 10, 1991

Michael says they play the game most every night at Blueberry Hill (the Vegas Denny's). Whether the winner or loser gets to go first next meal is up to house rules. It depends on how your peer group feels about the powerful staying in power. Don't worry about going first, it'll take six or seven times to hit.

It's a fun game, and remember to throw hard. You want that thing to explode when it's punctured (see pages 3–5). Really heave that little sucker. If you're worried about messing up the restaurant and causing more work for the innocent server or bus person, don't sweat it, almost all the coffee whitener gets absorbed by the loser's clothing. The little that hits the floor can be cleaned up with a napkin. It's just the right amount of mess to humiliate the loser and cause no one else any trouble. The later at night you play it and the farther from home you are, the funnier it is. This is entertainment for professionals.

More than limos and *Entertainment Tonight*, this game is pure showbiz. If you wonder what your idols are doing at any given time, it's a pretty safe bet that Slash is throwing a creamer at Axl's fork. Don't believe the hype.

SALT IN THE WOUNDS OF CREDULOUS FOOLS

For the human race to learn, everyone should honestly and patiently present the truth as he or she sees it. We should all listen to other points of view with an open-minded polite skepticism. Every individual should try to make sure that his or her facts are correct and when the facts contradict beliefs—the beliefs should be changed. The changing of beliefs to fit the evidence should be done with a smile and a celebration of real growth. We should all gather together on the shoulders of the giants that have gone before us, look around, and use our heads.

But...sometimes, we start to crack.

How many times can we say:

"Yeah, but extraordinary claims require extraordinary evidence."

How many times can we say:

"I don't have to prove there's no chance it DOESN'T exist— believers have to prove it DOES exist. You can't prove a negative."

How many times can we say:

"I understand that it SEEMED to work for your headache, but who was your control group?"

How many times can we say:

"Just because you, Geraldo, and the National Enquirer can't explain it, doesn't mean it's unexplainable."

How many times can we say:

"Real scientific breakthroughs are rarely first announced on TV chat shows by washed-up dancers."

—Huh?

Some people will just continue to believe that the check is in their mouths, no matter how much truth you put in front of them. That's no reason to get mean. Getting mean doesn't accomplish anything.

But, once in a while, when you're out with friends of friends, and the conversation has moved from UFOs to Elvis sightings[1] to ESP to "scientific" creationism to Paul McCartney being the most talented Beatle, it's time to switch to a policy of intellectual scorched earth—just for kicks.

When that time comes, the following trick will be eager to serve:

A big part of nonsense centers around healing. Everyone wants to be healed and no one wants to believe that even the tiniest ailment is with them forever. Every malady does one of three things if left untreated:

1. It gets better.
2. It stays the same.
3. It gets worse.

After trying any bogus treatment, one of three things will happen.

1. It'll get better.
2. It'll stay the same.
3. It'll get worse.

As long as you have a spiel for each of these three eventualities, you can be a healer that some people will believe in:

1. "See I told you."
2. "We arrested it."
3. "I guess we need more of it."[2]

Because everyone wants hope and it's easy to explain any course an affliction may take, there are many many cures that people believe in.

Here's a cure that works right in front of the suckers' eyes, right at the dinner table.

When the pseudoscience talk has pushed you over the edge, excuse yourself from the table. Once away from the cretins, pull a salt shaker from another table and dump some loose salt into your pocket or purse.

---

[1] This would be Elvis Presley. Elvis Costello sightings, although more rare, are still wonderful.

[2] If the person gets worse enough to die, you have "They got to me too late."

Take out a key with a round hole for the key chain. If you push the hole of the key against the tip of your finger and hold it there, hard, for a few seconds, you'll get what looks for all the world like a burn blister. You can set this up out of sight of the table, or if you just keep a little mystic-looking package of salt in your pocket or purse, you can make the "blister" below the table while they're still yapping, and you don't even have to get up.

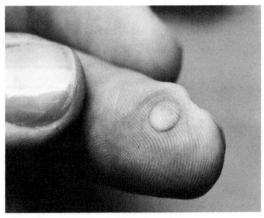

With some salt in the pocket and a "blister" on your finger, you're ready to rock. Spot something really hot at the table, we mean temperature hot, like a candle. A candle is perfect, but if there isn't a candle, you can use a match, or a lighter. Or, in a Mexican restaurant, you can try to time it so that when they say "Watch the plate, it's really hot" you have your blister and salt all ready.

Let's say it's a candle. Reach over for something in the middle of the table, pretend to brush the "blister" finger against the side of the candle,[3] and scream. Don't overdo it, one single-syllable obscenity should do just fine.

Pull your finger back and look at the "blister." Make sure everyone sees it. Say, "I used to hate little burns like this, until I got some of this homeopathic,[4] holistic,[5] Eastern[6] healing powder."

Reach into your pocket or purse (or better yet, your little mystical manila envelope—we gave you the label (see page 156) in the Gimmicks envelope, just stick it on) and pull out some grains of salt.

Rub the salt on your "blister" while you say, "There's a big conspiracy[7] to keep this stuff off the market in the U.S. Drug companies don't want it out because it cures every sort of skin problem and skin problems are big money for the Pig Power Structure Corporations.[8]"

By this time, the "blister" will be gone (it's the rubbing that does it). Show your finger around and say, "See? It works great."

Now you can be content with the satisfaction of knowing you've taken people whose world view is distorted and pushed them a little further into madness or, if that's not enough, you can take their money.

Offer to sell them some homeopathic,[4] holistic,[5] Eastern[6] healing powder for as much as you feel the market will allow. Give them a few precious grains of salt.

Now you've pushed them into madness, taken their money, *and* gotten them to rub salt in their wounds—literally. BTW—make sure you tell them it cures herpes.

We *are* the lowest of the low.

---

[3] **Don't really touch a hot thing with your bare fingers.** (Saving our collective ass from lawsuits sure is embarrassing.)

[4] This means there's nothing useful in it.

[5] This means nothing.

[6] Penn & Teller live around NYC.

[7] One of the more popular New Age nut concepts. (See page 43.)

[8] Same as above.

IT'S ABOUT TIME YOU GOT TO KNOW YOUR PIZZA PERSON

Some people have the phone number for their favorite pizza delivery joint scrawled on the refrigerator, some have it on speed calling, and some have it memorized. The best of us have all three. But for all the pizza you eat, when's the last time you spent quality time with the chef who cooks your pizza? What do you know about how your pie is prepared besides "600 degrees kills anything"? It's about time you took a little field trip to your true nutrition epicenter and

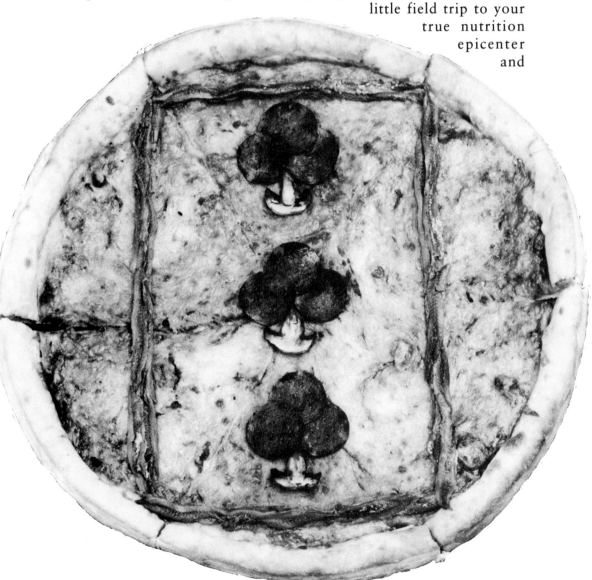

while you're there, set up the next trick. That's right, we're asking you to do something you may have never done before—we're asking you to *go to your pizza place in person.*

You're going to ask the big cheese who spreads the sauce on your pie to do you a favor. Don't worry, it's a small favor, and you'll have a note from Penn & Teller to break the ice. The note is on the opposite page. You can either Xerox[1] it or just rip it out of the book. Neatly fill in the blanks...and bring it to your pizza joint. You can't just drop it off, you have to find the most important pizza person, talk to him or her and leave the note stuck on the wall.

Once you and the pizza people are in cahoots and our note is on the wall, the hard part of the trick is done. All you have to do is learn the "All-Purpose-Penn-&-Teller-Play-With-Your-Food Three-of-Clubs Card Force" on page 25. You got that?

Okay, the next time you have friends over and the time comes for pizza, call your new pizza-buddies and order your pizza with the "P&T crust." If the person answering the phone doesn't know what you're talking about, tell them to read the "If Someone Asks for P&T Crust" note on the wall (you'll know where it is, you stuck it there). If one of your friends overhears you and asks what the hell "P&T crust" is, tell them it stands for "perfect and thin" (yeah, we know it's weak, but no one will ask). Wait a few minutes after ordering (wouldn't it be great if you could time it so you finished the trick just as the pizza arrived?) and do the "All-Purpose-Penn-&-Teller-Play-With-Your-Food Three-of-Clubs Card Force" (pages 25–34). Pick any card out of the deck *except the Three of Clubs*, show it to your friends and say "Is this your card?" It isn't.

When the pizza arrives, pay the guy (don't forget the tip). Let one of your friends take the pizza and as soon as they open the box yell, "Is that your card?" Don't snooze; you have to be on your toes and yell quickly. It's possible for hungry pizza lovers to rend a pizza illegible before noticing your card trick punch line.

---

[1] Xerox is a brand name (see the footnote on page 82).

TO MAKE A PIZZA WITH A P&T CRUST

Whatever toppings they order on the pie, arrange them so they form a THREE OF CLUBS (like the playing card).

Outline in some long thin topping like anchovies or green pepper (whichever they order)

Form each ♣ out of slices of pepperoni and mushroom.

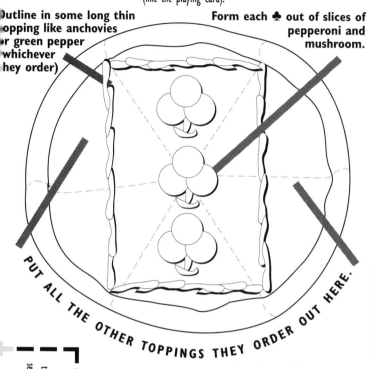

PUT ALL THE OTHER TOPPINGS THEY ORDER OUT HERE.

Dear Great Pizza Chef:

Hi. We're Penn & Teller, the guys in the picture. Maybe you've seen us on TV. We're personal friends with David Letterman, and we can tell you firsthand, that man loves good pizza. Your customer and our good friend _____ raves about your pies and orders from your fine delivery service all the time. We've taught _____ a magic trick that uses a pizza as a punchline. We'd be really grateful if you'd help make it work. All you need to do is this:

When _____ calls in and orders a "pizza with a P&T crust" arrange the toppings on the pizza like a playing card, the Three of Clubs. That's it.

And you can count on us to stop in for a slice the next time we're in town.

Gratefully, Penn Jillette & Teller

P.S. As a little token of appreciation, there will be an extra _____ bucks in the tip. That's for YOU. Don't forget to hit the delivery person up for your share.

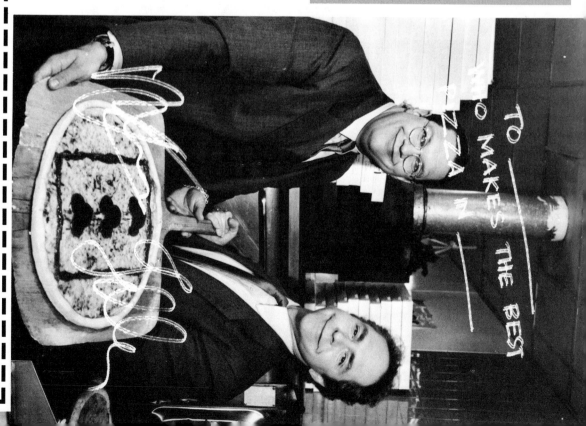

When you rip out this page and give it to your pizza chef, you will not be losing a thing except for this picture of a 1948 Buick.

A SCAM TO HELP WITH THAT PESKY COOKING MERIT BADGE

I was a Boy Scout. I only let this information out on a need-to-know basis. I'm not proud of it, but you need to know it for the next swindle. I was a Scout back in the good old days, back before all their time was spent keeping out Gays and Atheists; back when they still spent some time saluting and camping.

I think I got up to Life Scout. I think that's right below Eagle. If Eagle could have been bought with merit badges, I would have been a shoo-in. I had lots of merit badges, mostly goofy ones. All you had to do for the wacky badges was read the pamphlet, do one little project, and then go to some guy's house who was listed as an expert in that field. I got "Pets" (I kept a rabbit alive in a cage in my backyard), "Music" (I built a zither out of rubber bands and read music haltingly on the "Song Flute," a red plastic recorder), "Oceanogra-

phy" (I lived 120 miles from the nearest ocean, but I did my research at the local pond, close enough for the B.S.A.), and tons more. It was the irritating "Community and Church Service" that snatched Eagle from my deserving grasp—I just didn't do any. I do remember doing juggling shows at nursing homes that should have counted for something, but maybe that was later...I don't remember much about the whole Boy Scout experience. Some day I may reveal under hypnosis that these Scout memory blackouts are concealing a horrible experience with an older Scout or an alien ship or both together that has scarred me for life and made me the sick bastard I am today...or, more likely, I just wasn't paying attention. It's so hard to tell these days. The following story probably didn't even happen. I'm getting so I doubt everything.

No matter how many goofball merit badges you had there were specific ones required to move up a rung. I needed "Cooking." The cooking part of "Cooking" wasn't the problem (the phrases "Dutch oven" and "Poppin' Fresh" stick in my mind). The hard part for me was starting the goddamn fire. There was some stupid macho survivalist thing, involving three matches or something. You had to use birch bark to get it going, dry tinder and other stuff I just didn't care about. I needed a plan.

I decided to "Be Prepared." There was a place out in the woods a ways from camp where they gave the cooking tests. I took a little look-see out there on the morning of the day that I was to be tested. I took a Sterno can from under the urn that was used for the church "coffee hour." When I got to the clearing, I took the cover off the Sterno can, buried it in the ground, covered it with leaves, and put a twig over it so I could find the spot quickly under pressure.

When the time came I hiked out with all the fixins for dinner in my backpack (that was a requirement). The Scout Master took us to the designated clearing and ceremoniously handed me my three matches. I found my twig and started piling moist sticks on top of it in a haphazard way. It was a mess. The

Scout Master said, "I'm not really supposed to give you hints here, but I don't think that campfire design is going to work."

"I've had some luck with it in the past, sir." (It's often a good idea to use the word "sir" when you're a kid scamming an adult. It's amazing, but they don't see through it.)

"Okay. Good luck." He sighed and rolled his eyes.

What the Scout leader didn't know was that I didn't need luck. I had Sterno! I lit the first match and slid it under my random pile of damp sticks. A clean blue flame came from under the sticks and, after a good long while, caught them on fire. It was a beautiful thing. The Scout Master was in awe. We ate the "Poppin' Fresh" rolls out of the "Dutch Oven" and I got my merit badge.

If you're a kid, and you're not gay, and you believe in god, and you want a "Cooking" merit badge (this is getting to be a very small subset of the Penn & Teller audience), I hope you find this trick useful.

"A Scout is trustworthy, loyal, helpful, friendly, courteous, kind, obedient, cheerful, thrifty, brave, clean and reverent."[1] Five out of twelve ain't bad. It's almost half (that's 41.67%). In baseball that would be batting .417 and I'd be in the Hall of Fame.

---

[1] I did this whole list from memory. I do remember something from my Boy Scout years.

HOW TO LOP OFF YOUR THUMB
AND MAKE PEOPLE SCREAM

If you leave a carrot on your desk for a week, it will start to feel exactly like human flesh.

What good is this?

Well, the major good is: If you keep a few human-fleshy carrots lying around and *Late Night with David Letterman* calls you on Tuesday asking if you can appear on Wednesday, you can say yes.

Most of the time we invent our own tricks, but this one we picked up from Martin Gardner.[1] He, in turn, learned about the fun of desiccated root-vegetables from one of his boyhood heroes, a warped and ingenious codger named Joe Berg, who ran a magic store in Chicago. Berg discovered he could produce some homemade Grand Guignol by carving up an old carrot to resemble a thumb and switching it in for the real thing under cover of a paper napkin.

Then, while a spectator held the tip of the "thumb" through the napkin, Berg whipped out a big pair of scissors and snipped right through. But could such a simple gimmick scare anybody as worldly as David Letterman?

Yes.

---

[1] Gardner is a sort of all-purpose sage who knows everything about everything. He's also the author of a very long shelf of superb books on magic, science, mathematics, philosophy, history, and literature. (His most famous is probably *The Annotated Alice*, an amazing edition of the Lewis Carroll classics with all the background a modern reader needs to get the jokes.) His *Encyclopedia of Impromptu Magic* is the most useful book a food-player could possess. Except, of course, for this one.

PREPARATION

1. About a week before you think you'll need it, take a nice fat carrot out of the refrigerator and leave it on the coffee table (or your bureau, or your desk at work) to dry. If people ask what it's for, tell them it's a natural hygrometer.

2. The day before you plan to do the trick, take a small pair of scissors and cut the carrot to be the length of your extended thumb *plus three quarters of an inch*. Shape one end of it to resemble your thumb. Feel it. If it feels plausibly like flesh on bone, it's ready.

3. Right before you expect to perform, lay a large paper napkin nearby. Place the carrot underneath the napkin corner nearest you, and the part of the carrot representing the tip of the thumb pointing toward you. The napkin corner just barely hides the carrot.

4. Place a big pair of scissors ready and nearby.

PERFORMANCE

1. Ask your friend, "Are you familiar with the Ozark folk cure for arthritis?" If he/she says "Yes," get a new friend. If she/he says "No," proceed to step #2.

2. "Well, suppose your thumb stiffens up like this," you continue, sticking out your left thumb at right angles to your fist, as if hitchhiking. "Imagine it's throbbing and you can't stand the pain.

3. "Ozark folk healers just cover it with a rag—let's use this napkin..." With your right hand pick up the paper napkin by the corner, pinching the carrot behind it. Drape the napkin over your left hand, and as you do so, fold your left thumb inside the left fist and grip the piece of carrot in its place.

NOTE: Be sure you are not between the viewers and the light or they might see the silhouette of the exchange.

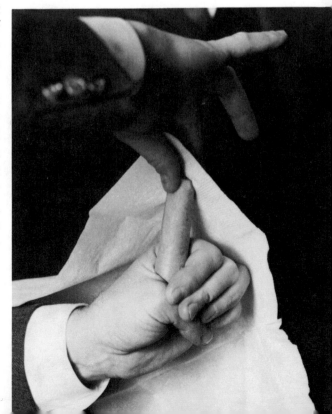

4. "...and ask a healthy member of their clan to take a firm grip on the tip—go ahead, grab the end of my thumb through the napkin..." Point to the end of the carrot. Your friend grabs it and holds it firmly.

5. "Then they wrap it nice and tight..." Use the right hand to gather the napkin around the fist, forming a loose cone with the tip of the carrot at the top. Pinch the gathered folds of the napkin between the tips of the left fingers and the base of the left thumb. Be careful not to wrap too tight, or the viewer might notice that the base of your "thumb" is in the wrong place.

6. Rotate your hand so that the carrot-thumb now points toward the spectator holding it, and say, "...and send for the blacksmith..."

7. Suddenly reach for the scissors, adding, "...who takes the tinsnips and..."

8. Snip through the carrot, leaving the tip in the spectator's hands. You will find that you never need to finish that last sentence, as your victim will be too busy screaming and throwing the "thumb tip" across the room.

NOTE: Don't cut off your friend's fingers or your own. You'll get no sympathy from us; in special effects, as in dueling, the participant who gets hurt the least wins. David Copperfield (the entertainer, not the waif) once inadvertently chopped off the tip of one of his own fingers while trying to cut a rope in half with scissors (a tool with one too many moving parts for David). He then went on a New York television show and made a big fuss about how his boo-boo proved that he was tougher than Penn & Teller. We said on the same show (between guffaws) that he could whittle off his arm with his nail file and still be a wimp. Don't confuse macho with muffed motor skills.

HIS SATANIC MAJESTY'S BURRITO

Nuts, particularly religious nuts, *love* the idea that their savior is lurking everywhere: in tortillas, billboards of spaghetti, even refrigerator mold. We think the Devil deserves equal time in the kitchen.

In this trick you make the hazy imprint of Satan's face appear on a tortilla right in your own microwave oven.

SECRET PREPARATION

Sorry to disappoint you, but it's just a trick. If there were really a Devil, and if we could get him do this stunt, we wouldn't be eking out a living writing family fun books. But this is quite a weird mystery and worth the preparation:

1. Get a package of tortillas (we prefer corn); some red, green, and yellow food coloring; and a small paintbrush.
2. Mix a drop of red, a drop of green, a drop of yellow, and two drops of water together in a saucer. This makes a kind of pale, murky brown that will pass for discoloration in the tortilla. Dip your brush and get a *small* amount of the dye on it. Wipe off any excess: the brush should be just damp with the color.

3. Paint a demon face on one side of your tortilla.

- Use just the tip of the brush, and dab it on little by little.
- *Don't* draw in big, bold lines; make it look as though it appeared from Hell, oozing out in little pools that just happened to come together to form a face.
- Remember: Keep your brush barely damp. If you slosh the color on in big, wet brushloads, it will soak through to the other side and give the trick away.
- Leave a good wide margin of space around your devil face. This will make the tortilla easier to handle without prematurely exposing your punch line.

4. Let the tortilla dry. Then put it back, picture side down, on the top of the stack of tortillas in the package. Return the package to the refrigerator.

5. Make sure you have handy a roll of waxed paper, a felt-tip marker, and a jar of tarragon or some other creepy-looking dried spice.

This devil-head will show you where your painting of His Infernal Majesty is at each step

Satan in the fridge, waiting for the trick to begin.

PERFORMANCE

This trick is not difficult to do. You don't need dazzling digital dexterity. But, unlike some of the other tricks in this book, you will need to rehearse this one several times *without an audience* until you are sure you have the whole sequence memorized.[1] Start with a few preliminaries:

1. Tell your friend you want to show her/him how diabolists use the microwave oven to worship Satan. This sounds plausible. To most people the microwave is already demonic, since its waves are invisible, and invisible things give people the willies.

2. Get out the roll of waxed paper. Tear off a strip about ten inches wide and lay it on the counter.

---

[1] If you want a trick you can do with no practice, try "Linguini à la Stigmata" (page 69) or "Stabbing a Fork into Your Eye" (page 3) or "Credit Where Credit's Not Due" (page 72).

3. Open the refrigerator and look in, as if you are trying to decide what to choose. Choose the tortillas. Bring them to the counter and take them out of the package. Take off the top tortilla and drop it onto the waxed paper. (This leaves your demon on the bottom, against the paper.) Deal off a second tortilla on top of the first.

Now you are going to build suspense and make it seem realistic by "failing" a couple of times. At the end of the two "failures" your friend will be absolutely convinced that both sides of both tortillas are blank.

THE FIRST "FAILURE"

1. Pick up the waxed paper with the two tortillas on it and put it in the microwave.

2. Cook it on high power for six seconds. Take it out again. This does nothing at all but warm the tortilla a bit and set the stage for the drama to come.

3. Eagerly remove the top tortilla as though you expected to find something under it. Flip it over and look underneath. Look puzzled. Shake your head and say, "Hmm. I wonder what the problem is."

4. Drop the tortilla you are holding *on the counter beside the waxed paper.*

"Hmm. I wonder what the problem is."

5. Lift the tortilla from the waxed paper and *without turning it over* drop it on the tortilla on the counter. Point to the waxed paper and exclaim, "Oh, of course! I forgot the pentacle."

"Oh, of course! I forgot the pentacle."

6. Take out your felt-tip marker and draw a large pentacle (a circle with a five-pointed star inside) on the paper.

7. If your friend asks, "Hey, isn't that the sign of the Devil?" pretend you don't know. This will make your friend think you *do* know but have some unwholesome reason for not acknowledging it. Your friend will picture you naked, devouring live sheep by moonlight.

THE SECOND "FAILURE"

1. Pick up two tortillas together, set them back on the waxed paper, and return everything to the microwave. Heat on high power for six seconds. Remove.

2. Very dramatically lift aside the top tortilla and reveal the bottom one. Act really peeved that there has still been no change. Say, "I can't understand it. I haven't done any good deeds lately."

   Note: Do not show the underside of the top tortilla—that's where your picture is.

   "I can't understand it.
   I haven't done any good deeds lately."

3. Replace the top tortilla on the one on the waxed paper.
4. The psychology of all this failure: Your friend has seen you fail twice, and is beginning to suspect it's just a dumb trick that won't work. Your friend is getting sick of looking at blank tortillas and is starting to wish *something* would happen. He/she's on *your* side now. Furthermore your friend now believes he/she has seen both sides of both tortillas blank again and again.

5. Say, "Okay, there's one last thing I can try." Go to the spice rack and get the tarragon. Lift the top tortilla and sprinkle tarragon between the tortillas. Be a little sloppy and frenetic, as if you are angry things aren't working. Replace the top tortilla.

"Okay, there's one last thing I can try."

6. Say, "Oh, what the hell! Might as well put some underneath, too." Pick the tortillas up and flip them over together onto the palm of one hand (this maneuver brings your demon to the top side of the lower tortilla). Shake tarragon on the waxed paper.

"Oh, what the hell! Might as well put some underneath, too."

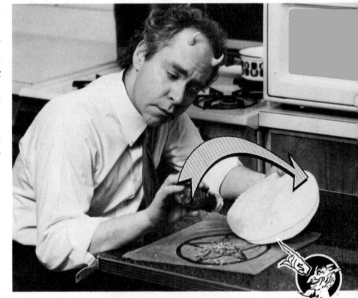

7. Keeping the tortillas in their new (flipped) orientation, replace them on the waxed paper and shake some tarragon on top. Say, "I'll be damned if this doesn't work."

"I'll be damned if this doesn't work."

THREE TIMES IS THE CHARM

1. Now for the socko finale. Put everything back in the microwave. Set it to cook for six seconds on high. Close your eyes and mumble, as if praying to Lucifer.[2]
2. When the cooking cycle ends, very gingerly take the tortillas out on the wax paper. Lift the top tortilla. Your friend sees the Devil staring him/her in the face. Reverently blow the tarragon off the picture, and throw yourself down in a kitchen chair, as if emotionally drained.

Your friend can examine everything, but there's nothing to find but a grinning Satan, creeping through the skin of a still-warm tortilla.

PARTING THOUGHTS

Rehearse this one. Don't just think about it; get some tortillas out and go through it step by step. It's just complicated enough that if you don't, you are likely to forget some crucial flip, blow the gaff, and end up in trickster's Hell: looking dumb while your friend laughs.

There are some places where this trick could get you killed.

The tortillas cook three times for six seconds. Six six six.

Loud, throbbing background music helps the effect. Try Carl Orff's "Carmina Burana," or Slayer's "Decade of Aggression."

Nothing about this trick requires a microwave. It will work equally well with a photocopier or waffle iron.

---

[2] If you want, you can chant in Latin, "Asso porco Diabolus gaudet," which means "The Devil enjoys roast pork."

HOW TO BE A GREAT OLDER RELATIVE

At age seven Teller visited his grandparents in Atlantic City. One day his grandfather took him out in a rowboat while his mother and father watched nervously from the dock. His grandfather gave him a string with a hook on the end, and Teller fished. He didn't catch any fish, but he did manage to drag out a huge clump of seaweed. His grandfather declared the seaweed a fine catch and brought it home.

That evening a large bowl of boiled seaweed had a prominent place on the table. Everybody had big portions and said they had never eaten finer. Even Teller—not exceptionally fond of bitter green vegetables—ate a plateful. Teller's grandfather had taught him to catch his own food, and as far as Teller was concerned, Pop-Pop was a god.

Extravagance is the hallmark of a great older relative. Such a person takes you fishing or to the movies; gives you brass dinosaur paperweights and money from foreign countries; knows all about tortures and perfumes and horse racing; and, naturally, does a few crazy tricks, tricks much too rude and silly for your parents, that *really* make you laugh.

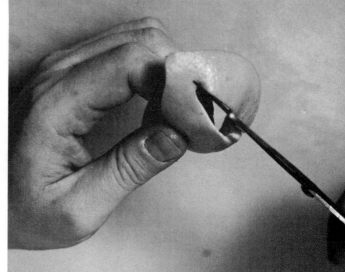

FUNNY ORANGE TEETH

1. Quarter an orange. Be careful to make your cuts from pole to pole (rather than through the equator).
2. Peel one quarter, being careful not to tear the peel. Eat the piece of orange. It's rich in vitamin C, which prevents scurvy. *Save the peel.*
3. Starting about one-half inch from the end of your piece of peel, make an incision down the center of the peel, stopping one-half inch before you reach the other end.
4. Make a series of little snips about one-quarter inch long and one-quarter inch apart along either side of the incision.
5. Turn the skin so that the albedo (the white fuzzy part) faces outward, and slip it under your lips.
6. Let your tongue run across the "teeth" and make monster noises.

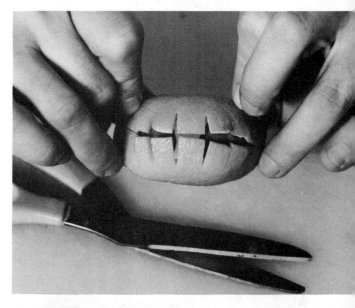

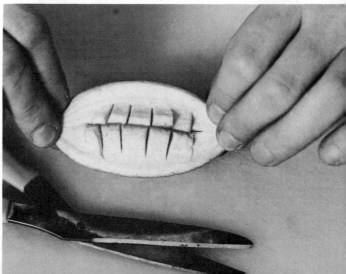

DIZZY EGGSHELL

1. Root through the garbage until you find a broken eggshell. This makes it already a good trick for kids.

2. Take a section from a gently curved side (rather than the end) and break off bits of the shell until you are left with a rough disc about the size of a half-dollar (a little over an inch; to non-Americans, three centimeters).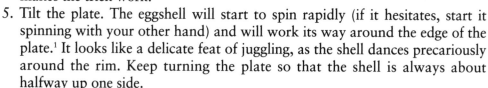

3. Get a smooth-surfaced china dinner plate and wet it under the tap. Make sure you moisten it all the way to the edges of the plate. Place the piece of eggshell on the plate, right at the edge.

4. Make music. Sing or whistle something fast and showbizzy. Get the child to sing along. Act as though the music is what makes the trick work.

5. Tilt the plate. The eggshell will start to spin rapidly (if it hesitates, start it spinning with your other hand) and will work its way around the edge of the plate.[1] It looks like a delicate feat of juggling, as the shell dances precariously around the rim. Keep turning the plate so that the shell is always about halfway up one side.

6. As you end the music, flatten the angle of the plate subtly, so that the shell stops spinning. Pick it up and make it bow, saying, "Thank you, ladies and gentlemen, thank you!" in your best eggshell voice.

[1] If for some reason your piece of shell doesn't behave as we describe below, you may need to try again with a different piece. Sometimes the balance is off just enough to keep the trick from working properly.

INTRAVENOUS GRAPE

1. When the child is looking the other way, *palm* a grape, like this, in your curved fingers.

2. Now with the same hand, visibly take a grape, and quickly toss it into your mouth *along with the hidden one.* Make a sour face and spit *one* out. Don't try to talk; make cave-dweller grunts.

3. Pretend to put the visible grape under the front of your shirt or down your blouse.[2] While your hand is under the shirt, palm the grape again and bring out your hand. From the back, your casually curved hand looks empty.

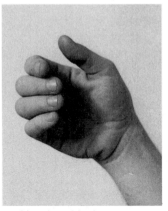 

Your hand looks empty.   *It's not.*

4. Immediately pretend to push the grape deep into your body. Imagine you are forcing it in through your navel. Use both hands. (NOTE: The grape is still palmed in the right hand.)

5. Now really go to town. Act as though you're using your hands to work the grape up through your stomach…into your chest…through your throat…

6. …and let it appear at your lips.

7. Kids will demand that you repeat the trick. No problem. Bring the hand with the palmed grape in front of your mouth. Pretend to take the grape out of the mouth, but really just suck it back in and show the one from your palm.

8. Repeat the trick. The more funny starting-places you can find, the better. For example, you might pretend to put the grape in your shoe and squish it with your foot, then appear to work it up the leg back to the mouth. No matter where you start it, be sure you use your fingertips to massage it along its imaginary course.

9. For a finale, hand the grape to the child and tell him/her to smash it as hard as possible right on the top of your head (sure, it will be a little fruity blob, but if you want to attain mythic status, you have to be willing to suffer). Pause. Look dazed. Then tilt your head back and spit the grape high into the air.

Kids will beg you to teach this trick to them. Don't. They really don't want to know.

Many summers after Teller's seaweed fishing trip, his grandmother confessed. She had taken the freshly caught seaweed from the murky Atlantic City harbor into the kitchen and switched it for some nice clean spinach she got at the produce market. All the adults had known the truth, but had played along to give the kid a thrill.

To this day, Teller never eats spinach without a twinge.

---

2   If your wardrobe or your ideals of deportment don't permit such actions, read on. Get the idea of the trick, and then choose a way to do it that fits your style.

In real life, we don't care for the idea of putting cyanide, arsenic, and other such condiments into co-workers' food. No matter how cleverly and wittily you commit it, actual murder is just unpleasant, not to mention illegal. You are much better off writing a story about it, which is exactly what we did.

Another Man's *Poisson*

- *I* -

Just looking at Mrs. Hooker, there was no way her students could guess she was a potential murderer. Sixty-two, rosy-cheeked, blond with only the tiniest hint of gray, she radiated scholarly enthusiasm as she addressed the four students in her Advanced Latin class.

"In the first three hundred lines of this play," she said, holding up a small black book with blood-red letters on the cover, MEDEA, "we see a woman deeply wronged. The tragic heroine, Medea, has given up everything for Jason, her husband. Then he turns right around and declares he's going to marry Creusa, the king's daughter. What do you think Medea will do?"

She took off her pink-rimmed glasses and leaned back in her chair, waiting. Through the open classroom window came the buzzing of a distant plane and a warmish breeze with a hint of hyacinths. It wasn't easy to concentrate on Seneca when spring smelled so good.

Karen Blanche raised her hand. "I bet she'll kill him or something."

"Really? Do you think she's capable of murder?"

Marty Marietta waved his hand. "Sure. Remember, she chopped up her own brother, just to help Jason escape. This girl's no dweeb."

"I see. Anyone else?"

Costa Areopolis raised a finger. "She's dangerous. She's got the power. She's a *venefica*. A witch."

"Origin of that word?"

"*Venenum*. Poison. As in 'venom.' She knows drugs. We saw that when she doped up that dragon so they could get the golden fleece. If I were Jason, I wouldn't mess with her."

"But if she's so dangerous, what do you suppose makes Jason think he's safe?"

A plump girl with dangling earrings and green eye shadow half raised a black-nailed hand.

"Yes, Ellen?"

"*A*: He's a man. *B*: He's good-looking. *C*: He's *really* self-centered—I mean all that matters to him is sex, money, and power." The bell rang. But in Mrs. Hooker's room, one did not move until she dismissed the class. So Ellen continued, "And *D*: Medea made the mistake of falling for him. So he thinks she still loves him, even though he's a rat."

"Exactly. And what do we call this smugness, this overconfidence, this tragic flaw?"

In unison, the class answered, "Hubris."

"Correct," said Mrs. Hooker.

- 2 -

Berenice Hooker had lived through a good many teaching nightmares in her twelve years as head of the Foreign Language Department: the girl who blamed her pregnancy on Mr. Mendoza's Spanish tutoring; the swastika Ms. Schoenberg, the German teacher, found spray-painted on her Volkswagen; the member of Berenice's award-winning Latin club—*Milites Linguae Virgilis*, the Soldiers of the Tongue of Virgil—who was bitten by a rat outside the Coliseum of Rome on a club trip.

But her present nightmare was a teacher.

His name was Mr. Roland Gotti, and he claimed to teach French—though in Mrs. Hooker's opinion, Mr. Gotti's classes would have learned more French eating deep-fried potatoes and visiting dry cleaners. Gotti's idea of a lesson was Edith Piaf on the hi-fi and a slide show of bikini-clad babes on the Riviera. It did not take a student long to realize that Mr. Gotti's three favorite French words were *hot dog*, *pique-nique*, and *blonde*.

Gotti would never have come near Berenice's department—an island of old-school excellence in a sea of TV-generation mediocrity—if he had not been the brother-in-law of the principal, Mr. Sturges. But Sturges had seized the opportunity to do some "emergency" hiring when the previous French teacher died in a collision with a limousine on New Year's Eve.

He explained his choice to Berenice. "Rolly Gotti isn't one of your halls-of-academe types, but *you* can show him the ropes. I'm confident he's got the makings of a great teacher: kids just naturally take to him."

He was right about that. Gotti was a big, handsome fellow with the lovable look of an athlete gone to seed. In his day he had been a rugby player. Girls found him irresistible. Boys, especially the kind who regarded school as a low-security prison whose only value was that it kept them from having to find a job, instinctively felt that here was one teacher who could understand what "putting in their time" meant. On top of that, Gotti was an easy grader, so kids knew he recognized talent.

His invasion of Mrs. Hooker's pedagogical paradise was made worse by the knack he had for putting a good face on his shenanigans. Berenice's head throbbed when she recalled the afternoon she had cornered him by the drip coffee-maker in the Foreign Language department office and told him in no uncertain terms that he had better start teaching French. Unruffled, he took his mug from its hook over the washbasin and poured himself a cup of end-of-the-day muck from the bottom of the pot.

"Bernie," he said with a sad little smile, "a great teacher of teachers wrote, 'The stage of romance must precede the stage of precision.' Very few of these kids are ready for precision. So I stick to the romance." He raised his mug in a toast, turned on his heel, and walked out.

Mrs. Hooker did not know which maddened her most: the smile, the sophistry, or the mug. Each teacher in her department had a recognizable coffee mug: Im Himmel gibt es kein Kaffee, In Heaven there is no Coffee, identified Ms. Schoenberg's. Mr. Mendoza's had a weeping Virgin. Berenice's, a gift from the Soldiers of the Tongue of Virgil, read Dux Intrepida, Fearless Leader.

But Roland Gotti's mug had not been presented by admiring students. He had bought it in a joke-shop. It had a badly drawn cartoon of an office-worker dreaming about a fish. It read: I'd Rather Be Fishin'.

And if I have anything to say about it, Mrs. Hooker thought, that's exactly where you'll be.

- 3 -

"Well, *bonjour!*" said Mr. Sturges, the principal, as Berenice caught up with him on his way to the parking lot. "Just the person I've been wanting to talk to." He was tall and slim. His shiny dark brown hair gleamed like the back of a beetle. He was carrying his briefcase in one hand, and had slung his overcoat over the shoulder of his beautiful navy-blue suit.

"I wonder if we could talk for a few..."

"Of course!" He sniffed the spring air. "*Voilà le printemps!* Eh?" he said, leading the way to a bench next to a plot of tulips. "Sit down, *mon amie.*"

"It's about Mr. Gotti."

Sturges seemed full of excitement. "*Mais oui!* But first let me tell you: You..." he said, taking both her hands, "are astonishing. I thought I had taken a chance bringing in Rolly in the middle of a school year—I mean, he's relatively new to the French game—but thanks to your help—do you know I've had over fifteen calls in the past month? *Fifteen calls* from grateful parents! 'My little So-and-so was failing French and now it's his favorite subject.'" He released her hands and began searching in his briefcase.

"Really, Mr. Sturges, you mustn't take..."

"Don't be modest, Bernie." He pulled out a computer printout. "Look at these grades. All 'A's and 'B's from kids who have never gotten above a 'C' in any class in their career. The man's a miracle worker. And I, for one, think it's largely your doing."

"Well, thank you. But I'm afraid there's a problem."

"A problem? Some smart bastard giving him a hard time?"

Berenice squared her shoulders. "Forgive me, but someone has to tell you. I'm afraid you've been misled about Mr. Gotti."

Sturges froze. "In what way?"

"Mr. Gotti is a popular teacher, but not a good one. To be perfectly frank, he is not even a bad one. He is not a teacher at all. He plays music. He tells stories. He's delightfully entertaining. But the students are not learning to speak French."

"Not learning...!" He held up the printout. "How do you explain these?"

"Arbitrary grading." She bowed her head. "He makes them up."

"And the calls from parents?"

"They know only what their children tell them." She slowly looked back up at him. "I'm sorry. I should have talked to you weeks ago, but I thought I could solve the problem on my own." She shook her head. "Nothing works. I've tried criticizing, praising, even planning lessons with him. It just rolls right off his back. With that kind of attitude I doubt Roland Gotti will ever become a competent teacher."

Sturges latched his briefcase. "I'm terribly disappointed to hear this from you, Mrs. Hooker." He rose, picked up his overcoat, and began to walk toward his car.

Berenice followed. "With your permission, Mr. Sturges, I think I should start looking for a replacement tomorrow..."

"You'll do no such thing." He turned and faced her. "Do you *really* imagine that I sit in my office, read grade lists, and chat on the phone with parents without checking into the operations of my own school?"

Berenice shook her head.

"Or do you think I've been away from the classroom so long that I've forgotten what matters in a teacher? Well, *I have not.* I've seen Roland Gotti in action. He may not be drilling constructions as much as you'd like, but he's teaching those kids to *think.*" He turned and started toward his sporty yellow sedan.

"Of course I respect your judgment, Mr. Sturges, but are you aware that in a normal language class, the students would already be..."

"'Normal'? Gotti's problem is not with teaching. It's with *you,* with your obsession with cookie-cutter standards. He's challenging your authority and clearly you don't like it!" He opened the car door and got in.

"That's not true. He's dishonest."

Sturges looked up coldly. "Mrs. Hooker: You are the head of the Foreign Language department—*at present at least.* This does not entitle you to call a teacher 'dishonest' just because he is more popular than you, or because he dares to do things a little differently. *Vive la difference! Comprenez?*"

He slammed the door, started the engine, and roared away.

Berenice stood and watched. Four words circled in her mind.

At. Present. At. Least.

- 4 -

Two miles south of the school, hidden away at the back of a motel parking lot, was a grimy orange neon sign depicting a bird on a buccaneer's shoulder. Teachers, mostly male, stopped in at The Hummingbird after school to talk sports and drink the tropical concoctions of an old Jamaican bartender named Doris. The drinks were strong and the decor simple: rattan furniture, a lacquered marlin, and a big plywood plaque jigsawed into a map of Jamaica and decorated with paintings of ugli fruit, hummingbirds, and Bob Marley. Above the bar was a television with the sound turned off, perpetually tuned to a channel on which preachers explained metaphysics with the aid of chalkboards and children.

It was a rainy Monday evening, a week after Berenice's disturbing chat with Sturges in the parking lot. At the bar Rolly Gotti was sitting alone, watching Doris with a glass of gin in her hand, who, in turn, was watching the television. A yellow-haired preacher in a blue seersucker suit was yelling into the red face of a woman in a wheelchair.

The sleigh bells hanging from the door clanked. Rolly looked around. It was Mrs. Hooker, in a red raincoat, dripping.

"Berenice! *Bonsoir.*"

"Hello, Roland." She looked the place over: bamboo, beads, fish, TV, Doris. "May I?" she said, indicating the stool next to Rolly.

"*Mais oui.* Drown your cares in a tropical treat?"

"Why not?"

Doris scrutinized Berenice. "Take your coat off, young lady. Let Doris make a nice hot rum toddy."

"Actually, I'd rather coffee, if you have it."

"Coffee? You *know* this girl, Rolly?"

Rolly hung Berenice's coat on a peg. "Know her! She's my one and only—if you don't count my wife and my Caribbean paramour." He reached across the bar and patted Doris on the hip.

"Sex-crazy!" she said, swatting his hand away. She picked up her gin and exited through the beaded curtain behind the bar.

Rolly pointed to the TV. The red-faced woman was struggling to arise from her wheelchair. "It's a trick," he said. "I read about it. The preacher has ushers who pick out anybody who walks with a limp and offer them front-row seating—in wheelchairs. Then when the show starts and the preacher gets them to stand up, it looks like a miracle."

"Disgusting."

"No, great. They're believing what they want to believe. They're happy."

"But it's dishonest."

"Like me?"

Berenice looked at the lacquered fish.

"Don't be embarrassed. Sturges told me that you thought I was dishonest because I gave high grades and didn't cover the material." He grinned. "Yep. I'm dishonest."

He was Irish-Italian with a broad face, straight, black, heavy hair loosely parted, eyes wide apart and tilted slightly, as if meditating on a joke. No wonder the girls were ga-ga.

"But I just can't bring myself to pretend that school will affect the rest of these kids' lives," he added. "When they're grown up and packing fried chicken in takeout buckets, who cares if they once could conjugate *avoir*?"

"Then why teach?"

"Why not? I work six and a half hours a day five days a week all winter long and get the summer off to go fishing. The kids love me, and old Sturges and I get to have the occasional beer and make fun of his sister. How many working people get this much profit on the sale of their soul?"

"There's something you're not telling me."

He furrowed his brow. "I don't think so. No."

"Yes. What is it that you long for, Roland?"

"Oh, that. Very perceptive. All right, yes."

"Tell me. What's your impossible dream?"

"Pretty standard." He shrugged and pointed to the cutout plywood map of Jamaica. "An island someplace. Running a nice little charter sailboat for millionaire fishermen whose yachts are in the shop. Eating jerk shrimp in a seaside shack. No grades. No lesson plans. No department heads." He winked at Berenice.

"Sounds perfect."

"Right. Just quit my job, leave my wife, grow a beard, forge a passport, and disappear on the next flight to Montego Bay."

"You wouldn't have to grow a beard."

Rolly laughed. "No thanks, boss. A hummingbird in the hand, you know."

Berenice took off her pink-rimmed glasses and set them on the bar. "Look at you. Halfway through your life, and your plan is to waste the other half doing what means nothing to you? Ten months a year walled up in a concrete block suburban tomb? 'Here lies Roland Gotti, who was never there.'"

He was suddenly serious. "I can't just..."

She grabbed his shoulder. "Why? You have nothing to lose but your roll-book. Write a letter of resignation. Throw a month's worth of clothes into a suitcase and hop on the next flight to the islands." Rolly stared into his glass. "Take your wife along. You both get jobs at a hotel until you find the boat of your dreams. Back here your brother-in-law sells the condo, sends you the check, and *voilà,* you're a charter service. You hang around the hotels, meet rich tourists, and turn on the patented Gotti charm. You do the booking, your wife does the books, and before your know it, your life is marlin and mangoes. Damn the bird in the hand. Damn the rules. Damn me. Do it!" Rolly sat unmoving, eyes closed.

The beaded curtain clattered as Doris pushed it aside. She set a small earthen mug of coffee on the bar. "There you are, young lady. Some rum in it maybe?"

For an instant, Berenice looked away from Rolly. "No, thanks." She turned back, but the spell was broken. Rolly was smiling a big, sad, we're-all-in-this-together smile. She almost knew what he was going to say.

"Nice try, Bernie." He put an arm around her. "Really nice try. Cicero would have been proud."

- 5 -

"'She seizes the death-bearing herbs, squeezes out the venom of the serpents, and mixes in filthy birds and the heart of a horned owl and the extracted guts of a living hoarse screech owl.'"

"Almost. Catch the nuance of holding the word *vivae* until next to last."

Mrs. Hooker's class was translating. They were approaching the climax of the play, in which Medea poisons her boyfriend's new bride, Creusa. Medea was just mixing the brew.

Marty Marietta nodded. "Okay. I see—the owl was still living when she gutted it. Cool. So how about, 'a screaming screech owl's guts, torn out while it was alive'?"

"Correct."

"Excuse me, Mrs. Hooker," interrupted Costa Areopolis.

"Yes?"

"I hate to criticize Seneca, but this recipe—this brew of death and destruction—just wouldn't work."

"Why not?"

"Simple. If you don't get snake venom into the bloodstream, it's useless; and as far as I can tell, she's not going to attack Creusa with a hypodermic. The dirty birds and owl guts sound disgusting, but in those days they didn't even know about bacterial infections. On the other hand, they did know about organic neurotoxins."

"Such as?"

"Well..." He reached under his chair, pulled out a shoe box and took off the large rubber band that held it closed. "All she'd need is something like this." He opened the box.

Inside was a live toad the size of a Danish ham. The pale sac under its chin pulsed each time it breathed.

Mrs. Hooker said, "My god!" Karen Blanche screamed and stood up by the wall. Marty Marietta grinned. Ellen, the girl with the black fingernails, looked bored. "Oboy," she said, "let's bring in a frog and scare the girls."

"Toad. A marine toad, *bufo marinus*. And I'm not trying to scare anybody. He's harmless. Little girls in Australia keep them for pets and dress them up in doll clothes." Karen took a step away from the wall.

"But it's so *ugly!*" she said.

"That's what it thinks about *you*," said Marty.

Mrs. Hooker had pulled herself together. "Costa, this is very disruptive. You should not bring animals to class."

"But I thought it was relevant. I mean, *this* is something witches really used in brews. You see, toads have venom glands in their skin that make them poisonous to predators. It's a defense. It's been known for thousands of years. In fact, in Roman times, women used to boil

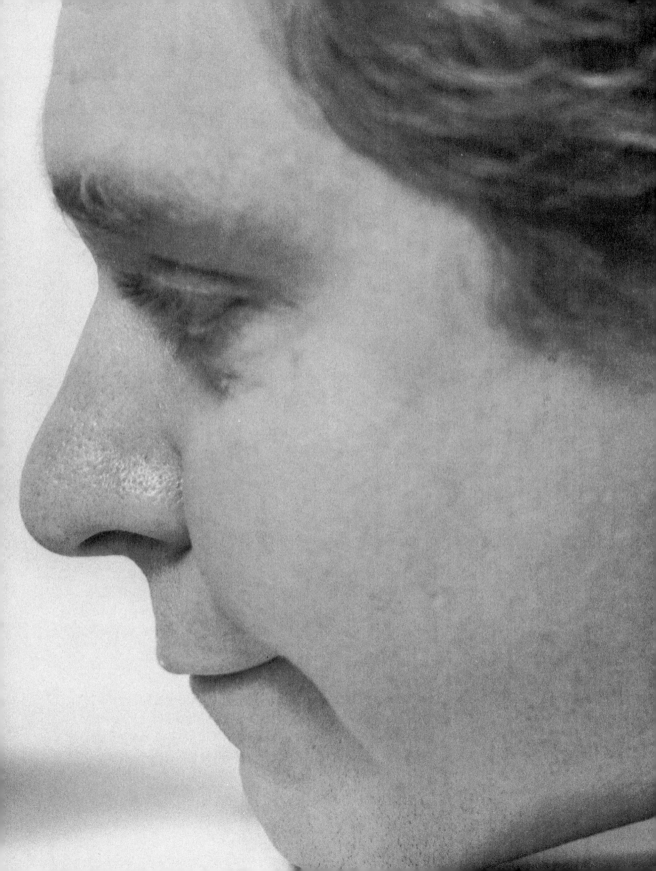

toads and use the extract to kill their husbands. It looked like a normal heart attack. So why does Seneca have Medea using snakes?"

Mrs. Hooker had no ready answer.

Marty Marietta could not contain himself. "Can I touch it? Jesus, how big *is* that sucker?"

"This one's only fifteen centimeters—around six inches—but they get a lot bigger. Don't squeeze it there," he said, pointing to a large bump on either side, just behind the head, then to others on the top of each hind leg, "or there. Those are the poison glands. If you do it just right, it'll squirt out quite a distance. Hit a mucous membrane, like in your eye, and you're in trouble."

"Costa. Put it away. Now!"

With a shrug, he closed the box, secured it with the rubber band, and put it back under his chair. Karen Blanche uneasily resumed her seat.

"Thank you." Mrs. Hooker took a breath and smoothed the jacket of her gray suit, as if wiping poison from her hands. "All right, now that show-and-tell is over, Costa, please explain your point again. You think Seneca should have Medea using toads in her brew?"

"Yes. See, I borrowed Jabba from the science lab over the weekend. Mr. Townsend gave strict instructions about caring for Jabba: she could stay in the box or in my terrarium, but she could not be let loose."

"It's a *girl*?" asked Karen, appalled.

Costa ignored her. "So I was doing everything according to the rules. I kept her warm, fed her earthworms—in the lab we give her crickets and goldfish..."

"Omy*god!*" said Karen and put her head on her desk.

"And everything would have been just fine. But then I made the mistake of letting my little sister pet her, and she kind of fell in love with Jabba, and took her out of the terrarium to play with her when I was washing the car, and..."

"And she squeezed the poison glands and blinded herself?" contributed Marty hopefully.

"Shut up. No, she let Jabba loose and was chasing her around inside the house. But you see, my dad just bought this golden retriever, and when the dog saw Jabba hopping by—well, he gave a snap and caught her in midair. He dropped her almost instantly and all of a sudden was lying on the floor with his legs spread out. My sister called me and my dad, but by the time we got there, the poor mutt was panting and his heart was beating like mad. His eyes were bugging out and it looked like his hind legs were paralyzed. Then he got really quiet and died."

Karen peered over her arm. "It *killed* your dog?"

"The toad didn't even have teethmarks on it, so I figured the dog couldn't have swallowed much venom at all. That made me think about poisoning and poisoning made me think about this play. So I looked it up and sure enough *veneficae* like Medea had been milking toads and murdering people for centuries, and that made me wonder why Seneca had Medea using snakes instead of toads."

Marty broke the silence. "What did you do to your sister?"

Costa smiled. "Justice. I fed Jabba her hamster."

- 6 -

The airless environment of a school has a way of magnifying annoyances into problems, problems into obsessions, and obsessions into matters of life and death. And by late May, Roland Gotti had become Mrs. Hooker's obsession.

He seemed to be infecting everything she cared about with his warm, wise hopelessness. First Mr. Mendoza started letting his classes watch Spanish soap operas one day a week. "What's the point," he said, "of forcing grammar down their throats when most of these kids won't get any closer to Spain than a mall taco shop?" Then Marty Marietta and Karen Blanche elected to go on a weekend ski trip instead of attending the two-day State Classical Olympics. "What's the point?" they said. "We're the best. Why keep proving it?"

As Berenice slipped, Rolly seemed to climb. There was talk of him starting a rugby club. That got him a big interview in the school newspaper. She noticed Sturges was giving Rolly a lift home every afternoon. Then one morning at the beginning of the next-to-last week of school, Ms. Schoenberg, the German teacher, came to Mrs. Hooker before First Period began and asked if Berenice were really going to resign as head of the Foreign Language department. She was stunned. Where had Ms. Schoenberg heard such a thing? "That's just what everybody's saying," Ms. Schoenberg shrugged.

That day Berenice's first two classes went by in a red blur. By Third Period she found herself bumping into the blackboard rail and calling students by the wrong names. Fourth Period—her free period—came at last, and she fled to the Foreign Language department office. She lay down on the faded red vinyl couch, put her wrist over her eyes, and fell asleep.

She dreamed. Roland Gotti was a naked slave dancing on the middle of a Roman banquet table. As he twisted and turned, his body gleaming with sweat, Doris, the Hummingbird bartender, stood up in a long red robe. She beckoned to him and offered a drink from a big pottery goblet made in the shape of a toad opening its mouth to the sky. Gotti the slave knelt before her. "Kiss the Devil," she said, raising the cup and pouring luminous green liquid down his waiting throat. There was a sizzling sound and yellow smoke billowed from his mouth. Then as the crowd looked on, the body of the naked slave burst into white flame and sank to the table, a lump of stinking, molten flesh.

Berenice awoke, breathing rapidly. She looked at the clock. It was Fifth Period, her lunchtime. Rolly's was Sixth Period. She stood up and smoothed her hair by the small mirror above the washbasin. Then she took Rolly's I'D RATHER BE FISHIN' mug from its hook and put it in her purse.

- 7 -

Mrs. Hooker stood in the empty corridor, looking through glass panels in the door of the science lab. Mr. Townsend had left for lunch. The door was locked, but years ago the janitor had made her a copy of the master key. She unlocked the door, stepped inside, and locked it again.

Formaldehyde. She recognized the deathly smell. She could almost taste it.

The room was dark. The blackout shades were drawn and she could just make out the white rectangle of a small projection screen hanging at the front. She pulled down the shade on the door.

She moved in darkness now, tentatively, guided by the faint light that crept from around the edges of the shades, past the tall, padlocked closets at the back, then down the aisle between the lab tables. Each table had two pairs of rubber gloves and two metal trays, a large one half-filled with a gray, waxy substance, and a small one with knives.

Where are you, my slimy ally? she thought.

At the front of the room was a demonstration island with a deep stainless-steel sink. Behind it she could make out the lens of an over-head projector aimed at the screen hanging from the upper rail of the blackboard. At the window-end of the island was Mr. Townsend's desk, and on it a terrarium.

She clicked on a tiny lamp clipped to the front glass, and saw. All mouth and eyes on the body of a miniature wrestler, the toad sat staring like a warty buddha. Its only sign of life was the pulsing of the speckled sac in the front of its throat. Its front legs looked like muscular human arms, complete with hands with four little fingers. On each side, just behind the head, was a triangular lump the size of half a walnut; these were the deadly venom glands that had killed Costa's dog.

Taped in the corner of the front glass was a yellow cardboard tag, BUFO MARINUS—MARINE TOAD—'JABBA.'

There was no time to waste; the class period would be over in twenty-two minutes. Berenice took Gotti's mug out of her purse and set it on the desk. She unhooked the spring-steel clips that held the screen on the top of the terrarium and removed it. Then she picked up the mug and lowered it in, mouth down, rim aimed at the poison gland on the toad's neck.

The toad hopped.

It rammed its face against the front of the terrarium and scrambled with both its baby-wrestler hands against the glass. Berenice jumped back, her heart pounding.

She would need to hold the toad in place and squeeze the gland with her fingers, but the thought of touching the vile thing with her own flesh was more than she could stand. She remembered the latex gloves on the worktables. She turned, picked up a glove and pulled it on her left hand. There was a thud behind her.

She turned back. The terrarium was empty.

She scanned the top of the desk, then squatted. Holding her breath, she crouched lower, tentatively bringing her face to the dim gap between the bottom of the desk and the floor. The light from the window grazed the tiles. The toad was not there. It had to have gone behind the demonstration table.

She stood again and circled back around the front of the desk. She moved step by step, squinting into the darkness to see her feet. When she reached the overhead projector, she knelt next to it, located the switch, and turned it on.

The screen on the wall lit up. On it was the giant silhouette of a toad. She caught her breath and turned. The *bufo* was sitting on the glass surface of the projector, six inches from her face. She lost her balance and fell backward onto the floor.

The *bufo* hopped off the surface of the projector and across the demonstration counter into the sink. On the screen Berenice saw projected the transparency the toad had been sitting on: a photograph of a dissected frog with the exposed parts labeled: LUNG, LIVER, HEART.

She grabbed the corner of the counter and pulled herself to her feet. The light from the screen reflected off the bottom of the stainless-steel sink, illuminating the toad as with footlights. She took a step toward it. It hopped, struck the smooth wall of the deep sink, and bounced back inside.

"Too bad," she said. "You're trapped." She sucked in a breath between her teeth and lunged.

She had forgotten that her right hand was gloveless and for an instant she was startled to feel the cool, rubbery skin against her warm, bare flesh. But she did not let go. She gripped the animal with both hands and lifted it off the bottom of the sink. The toad reached out, paddling the air with its front and hind legs, helpless. The animal was weak and she was strong. It felt good.

She shifted her grip, and found she could hold it in just her right hand, dangling it from a hind leg, while with her left hand she retrieved the mug from Mr. Townsend's desk. She set it in the sink, then suspended the toad so that the poison gland was directly above the cup.

She squeezed the gland with her gloved left hand. The poison shot into the mug like a jet from a water pistol, spattering the sink and splashing her cheek and eyeglasses. Unflinching, she lifted the cup and looked inside. About a teaspoon of clear liquid was in the bottom. She sniffed. It was nearly odorless. It would easily pass for water left in the cup from its last rinse.

"Drown your cares in a tropical treat?" she whispered.

She looked at the clock. In seven minutes the bell would ring, but Mr. Townsend might return early. She lifted the *bufo* like a newborn baby and lowered it into the terrarium. She replaced the screened lid and turned out the light. She rinsed her eyeglasses, wiped her cheek, and swabbed the inside of the sink with a wet paper towel. She pulled off the rubber glove, tossed it into the garbage, and washed her hands.

Then Berenice picked up the I'D RATHER BE FISHIN' mug with its precious contents, and put it into her purse, cradling it carefully to keep it from spilling. Then she flicked off the overhead projector lamp, went to the door, raised the blackout shade, stepped out into the empty corridor, and relocked the door behind her.

Correct, she thought, as she hung the mug from its hook above the sink in the Foreign Language office. She had even remembered to wipe her fingerprints from the handle.

Correct. Medea herself could not have done it more neatly.

- 8 -

"Mrs. Hooker."

It was the next-to-last class period, Advanced Latin. Less than an hour to the end of the day. Gotti always dropped in at the Foreign Language department office after school for one final cup of coffee. He was nearly forty, she guessed. It would pass for a heart attack.

"'O Rage, where you lead, I follow,'" said Costa. "Is that okay?"

"Correct."

Karen Blanche raised her hand.

"Yes?"

"I know we've only got a couple pages to the end, but this is starting to seem like a cheap horror movie. I mean, I understand completely why Medea would want to poison her husband's girlfriend. She hates her. But why is she killing her own sons, too? I mean, sure, they're Jason's sons and it will make him feel awful, but won't it make *her* feel even worse?"

"She's out of her mind," suggested Marty. "Maybe she's been drinking too much of that brew with the owl guts in it."

Costa shook his head. "She's not thinking. She's acting on instinct, like an animal."

There was a silence. Mrs. Hooker looked over at Ellen, who was rubbing a pencil eraser along the ends of her black fingernails.

"I think," said Ellen, "it's like a divorce. If she gives her sons to Jason, he'll ruin their lives with his rotten values. She's a good mother. She thinks they're better off dead."

"Besides, it's a tragedy," added Marty, brightly. "Everybody's *supposed* to end up miserable."

The bell rang. Mrs. Hooker gave the homework assignment and the students filed out. "Excuse me," said Ellen, touching Mrs. Hooker's arm. "Nobody else would notice, but do you know you've got a rash on your cheek? I thought maybe you could use some lotion." She held up a small pink bottle.

Berenice touched her face where the venom had splashed.

"Thank you, Ellen, but it's just allergies."

When Ellen had left, Mrs. Hooker took the compact out of her purse and looked into the mirror. Three small patches on her face were blistered as if they had been scalded by hot fat. She dabbed the areas lightly with powder to hide the redness.

I'll go to the school library, she thought. *I'll be in the library when it happens. They'll call me, and I'll be looking for photos of famous productions of Medea. Yes, that's it, the library.*

She gathered her things and started down the hall. The door to the classroom where Gotti held his last-period class was open. Should she look in? Of course. She should glance in casually, just as she normally would.

The room was empty, except for one short, slender girl with her blond hair in a braid. She had her head on the desk. Berenice went in.

"Isn't there a class in here? Where is Mr. Gotti?"

The girl raised her head.

"Where is Mr. Gotti?" asked Berenice, firmly.

"Gone."

"Gone where?"

"Gone. He told us yesterday. He made us promise not to tell."

"Gone *where?*"

"Jamaica. He's never coming back."

"What?"

"He's going to Jamaica to buy a boat and go fishing with million-aires. He told us yesterday. He made us promise not to tell."

"Did he leave yet? Where is he now?"

"Meeting somebody. In the Language office, I think. He said he wanted one last cup of coffee for the road."

- 9 -

Berenice ran all the way to the Foreign Language department office. The door was closed and the shade was drawn, but inside she heard voices. The first was Gotti's, saying, "…and then she actually *served* it to us, completely convinced it was Spam!" Another man laughed and said, "A toast—to your sister, mistress of mystery meat!"

Berenice pushed the door open.

Gotti was standing with his back to Berenice. His head was tipped back and she could see the handle of a coffee mug in his hand. "Mmmm," he said, lowering his head. "Bottom of the pot. Deadly." She heard the clunk of the china as he set the cup on the window ledge.

She thought, *He's going to die.*

"Look, Rolly, your girlfriend's here!" said Mr. Sturges, lying on the red vinyl couch and pointing to Berenice with his cola can.

Gotti turned around. "Look who's here! Heard the news? I'm a ghost. Gone with the wind. Yesterday's muffins. *Au revoir,* academia!" He looked exuberant. Yesterday his complexion had been gray, but today he seemed to glow.

He snapped his fingers. "Yo, wake up! How about a little congratulating? You are looking at the new bartender of the Buccaneer Beach Hotel, Kingston, Jamaica. I fly out day after tomorrow with the little woman and the big suitcase. If that doesn't excite you, think of it this way: You're rid of me."

Berenice watched Gotti. There was nothing she could do. The venom would strike and he would die. It was too late. Any attempt to warn him or get medical help would only be a confession of murder. The only rational choice was to remain silent and as calm as possible.

Then she heard a voice say, "Roland, we have to call a doctor. We've got to get you to the hospital." She realized it was her own voice, the no-nonsense one she used when students were out of order in the classroom.

Gotti began to laugh. "I'm not crazy. I just know what I want." He put his big arms around her. "And what I want is a little serious congratulation." Still laughing, he put his hands on her hair, pulled her face to his and kissed her. She tasted his saliva. Bitter. Acidic. Venomous.

She pulled herself away, frantic. "No. Listen to me. You're going to die…"

"Get a grip on yourself, boss. I'm going to *live*—for the first time in my adult life. Before you came into the Hummingbird that night, I was dying. But nobody knew it. I had everybody fooled. Kids. Parents. Me. It still gives me the creeps to think that if you hadn't pulled your

Cicero, I would have died a little every day for the next thirty years—just like *him*!"

He pointed to a mug hanging over the washbasin.

Berenice looked, then looked again.

I'D RATHER BE FISHIN' was hanging right where she had left it.

Gotti took the mug off the hook and jabbed his finger against the cartoon of the deskbound man dreaming of the fish. "I'd have died a little every day, just like this jerk, for the rest of my life. But now, as far as I'm concerned, he's dead!" He heaved the mug into the big trash can by the copier. "So what do you— Hey, boss, what's the matter?"

Berenice had dropped her purse and was leaning on the radiator.

"Are you okay? You want me to make some fresh coffee...?"

She shook her head.

Rolly looked inquiringly at Sturges, who shrugged. "It's been a tough week for all of us," Rolly added gently. "These sexy May days are murder..."

But Berenice was not listening. She was staring at the mug on the window ledge, the mug Rolly had drunk from.

He grinned. "Pretty sweet, eh? The kids found it for me overnight. My going-away present." He handed it to her. "Turn it around. I bet you'll laugh."

She held the mug for a moment, then turned it.

It was another joke-shop special, much like Rolly's old mug. But the cartoon was different. It depicted an unoccupied desk stacked high with unfinished business. And tacked to the stack was a sign.

It read: GONE FISHIN'.

WHAT ABOUT SECRETS?

Why are magicians so nutty about keeping secrets? And should *you* be nutty about the secrets you learned from this book?

It's up to you, of course. We don't want to tell you how to live your life or use the information in this book (except to tell you to MIND OUR SAFETY WARNINGS). But deciding whether to explain a magic trick is an aesthetic/personal choice. It is not like selling military secrets in wartime. No infant has ever died of magic-trick exposure. Still, you should consider your goals.

If you want credit for being clever, you should probably not tell. Good tricks usually have dopey, unimpressive explanations. Look at the Letterman Fish/Watch Trick. If you saw us do the trick on TV, you probably thought we were amazing sleight-of-hand wizards. Then we told you how the trick was done, and you realized we were just liars willing to pay a man to hide in a table full of cold fish guts. Of course, we had a *reason* for telling you. We thought it made a good story. Good stories make good books, and people *buy* good books.

But let's look at "His Satanic Majesty's Burrito" (page 176), a trick you might be tempted to share with a friend. When you do this trick, the audience assumes you are either a science wiz who knows some really cool stuff about microwaves or in league with the Evil One. Either way, you appear to be a fascinating person. But if you explain the trick, suddenly they know you're just a twit who sits around the kitchen noodling with paintbrushes and food coloring. And don't imagine they're going to be blown away by the moves; flipping a tortilla is not an impressive skill.

So you can see why Houdini didn't give away tricks until he was good and ready. (He had a great habit of doing a trick until other magicians started to catch on and imitate him. Then he'd invent a cleverer method and go around "exposing" his original method as that of cheap impostors.)

But if you see an opportunity to make your life better by teaching somebody a trick, here are a few tips to keep you from kicking yourself later:

— If you teach a trick, go all the way. Make sure your friend actually learns to do it. Rehearse until she/he does the trick well. There are already more than enough incompetent magicians without your adding to the problem. But there's a side benefit: If you just tell somebody a secret, and that person does not actually perform the trick, he/she will be apt to shout out the explanation in the middle of *your* performance. This stinks. Whereas if your friend *does* the trick, she/he has an investment in keeping the knowledge out of the hands of the uninitiated.

— Get something you want in exchange for your secret. Information has value, and your friend will be apt to recognize this when he/she has to fork over money, goods, or services. Get a good price and you will be less apt to hear the sickening whine, "Oh, *that's* all it was. I thought it would be something *good,*" which invariably greets you if you cave in to idle curiosity for free.

— Follow the example of magic shops: They always say, "Give us your money first, *then* we'll teach you the secret." Collect up front, or expect to be stiffed when they find out how drab the real secret is.

But if you don't want to waste your time teaching or selling your secrets, what do you say when somebody asks, "How did you do that?"

Naturally, the best answer is "If you really want to know, go buy a copy of *Penn & Teller's How To Play With Your Food.*" But if you prefer to hoard your secrets and impede the advancement of Humankind through knowledge, that's your right.

In that case, when somebody says, "C'mon, tell us," say quietly but decisively, "No." If they ask why, explain that puzzling out magic tricks is good for them; it tests their powers of observation and stimulates their reasoning faculties (which is true). If they persist, shake your head and lament the deterioration of critical thinking in today's society.

If they still hound you, pretend to give in. Take the curious person into a quiet corner. Bring your lips to his or her ear. Then scream at the top of your lungs, "IT'S A TRICK!!!!" It helps make the point if you then pop in a set of "Funny Orange Teeth" (page 185) and roll around shrieking with laughter.

JOIN THE PENN & TELLER FAN CLUB

Send $6.00 to:

MOFO
P.O. Box 1196
New York, NY 10185

GOT A MODEM?

Call MOFO EX MACHINA, the bitchin'est BBS in the jungle.

- Just call 1-800-365-4636
- Hit ENTER twice
- Type the password MOFO

THANKS

Thanks from the bottom of our collective pumping heart to:

Mom & Dad Jillette and Mam & Pad Teller not because they are our parents but because they are the four best people on Earth, okay? You got a problem with that? They also gave us our lives, our personalities, our values and the stupid wizard and Boy Scout pictures.

Valda Stowe—she's Penn's sister and he calls her "Sister." She gave us the stupid pumpkin picture.

Carol Perkins. Support minus zero no limit.

Ken "Krasher" Lewis and Robbie Libbon—Penn & Teller are four people, these are the other two.

T. Gene Hatcher for Lord Kitchener's ants, and other juicy historical morsels; also, for quelling Teller's excessive assonance and alliteration.

Jamy Ian Swiss was creative consultant on this book, R&D&I (Inspiration). He is one of the best people alive with whom to have dinner. He's one of the magicians that we like. He also made sure the tricks in the book work and that proper credit was given. When we needed information on poisonous toads—he got it. When we needed a poisonous toad—he got it. There may be close-up magicians as good as Jamy but there is none better. If you're in NYC, see him do close-up—he'll kill you dead.

rob Pike, he's a good friend who finds lots of mistakes.

Elliot Freeman drew the pictures for the "The Story of Little Ginny Goblin and the Dancing Kandy Korn," a friend from a little before the word "go."

Mike Epstein—e-mail buddy who helped with lots of data on toads and stuff.

Ron Gomes is a friend who dressed up like a Rabbi and Julie Huss is a friend who dressed up as a vegetarian chef.

Peter Fitzgerald—"2 grey suits" and a coat full of treyf.

David Shaw and Diane Martin (a microbiologist and a lawyer under one roof. We have them on speed calling).

Trattoria Dell'Arte Restaurant in NYC featuring Sandra Scandiber—for good pictures and good food.

Jack Tillar, Academy Award winner and Emmy-winning composer, for the Blister Trick.

I. D. Abella, Alysia (House of the Redeemer), Jeffrey R. Appling, Scott Brigham, Harry Blackstone, Bronx Reptile, Steve "The Dootch"

Carduci, Alden Cohen, William B. Collins, Mrs. Philip Douglas, Famous Casa Nova Pizzeria Restaurant at 9th & 46th in NYC, Nancy Fitzsimmons, Martin Gardner (for knowing everything), Don Gardulo, Neil Gershenfeld, Eddie Gorodetsky (the funniest man in the world), Michael Goudeau, Jackie Green (the idea of making dessert bleed), Mike Hawley, Ellen Hovde, Aye Jaye, Maggie Jamroz, Joseph Edwards Jewelers, Mac King, Ray Mendez, Jay Marshall, Muffy Meyer, Stephen Minch, Scot Morris, MovieNight, Rich Nathanson, *New York* Magazine, Victor Pahuskin, The Residents, Susan Rice, Rosey, Rich Shupe, Gary Stockdale, Meredith Tanner, Johnny Thompson, Too Much Joy, Kathy Travers, and Michael McKenzie "Pie" Wills (he made a lot of bleeding Jell-O).

David Letterman, Robert Morton, *Late Night with David Letterman*, and NBC.

David G. Rosenbaum, David Glenn, and D. Glenn Ross for poetic underpinnings.

Craig, Flip, John, and Andrew at Pixar.

The Melon Shoot Shoot—Donna Crespo (The MovieNight Cop), Dave Lyman (Blue Trail Range in Wallingford, Connecticut), Herb Dalessandro (firearms and melon shooter—we pity the poor melon that tries to rough him up).

David Ben, Lucia Hwong, Tony Mackintosh, Alan Marke, Hedda Moye, Molly O'Neill, Meena Sud, Alice and Calvin Trillin, Ed Victor, Richard Ward, and T. Ted Wright for their connections in the restaurants of three continents.

The Jungle (Those people not previously thanked): Steven Banks, Alex Bennett, Chip & Grace Denman, Marc Garland, Tim Jennison, Gary Stockdale, Steve Strassman, Colin Summers.

The Try-Out-the-Tricks-Party (Those people not previously thanked): Jay Blumenfield, Elliot Brown, Robin Carrigan, Stephanie Long, Sal Longo, Maureen McMahon, Marcia Palley, Peter Schankowitz, Jen Weisel, Billy and Violet West.

James Randi, our hero, our role model, our friend.

THE PENN & TELLER TIME LINE

1948 February 14: Teller born in Philadelphia, PA.

1955 March 5: Penn Jillette born in Greenfield, MA.

1974 April 10: Penn meets Teller through Wier Chrisemer.

1975 August 19–September 3: Minnesota Renaissance Festival.

    October 9: "Asparagus Penn's Unicycle Jump for Life."

    November 4: First "Asparagus Valley Cultural Society" show at Princeton's Theatre Intime.

1977 January 11–January 30: "Asparagus Valley Cultural Society" at the Walnut St. Theatre in Philadelphia.

    March 10: "Asparagus Valley Cultural Society" makes its first television appearance on the "Mike Douglas Show."

1978 August 16: P&T's van is broken into and all their equipment is stolen.

1979 April 26: Opening of "Asparagus Valley Cultural Society" at San Francisco's Phoenix Theatre.

1981 October 31: Closing night at the Phoenix Theatre.

1982 January 22–March 14: "Mrs. Lonsberry's Seance of Horror."

    August 20–September 5: Minneapolis Renaissance Festival.

    September 9–October 3: Houston Renaissance Festival.

    December 1–12: "Penn Jillette and/or Teller" at The Comedy Cabaret in Minneapolis.

1983 August 19–August 28: Toronto: Canada's Wonderland.

    August 31–September 16: "Penn Jillette and Teller" at The Comedy Cabaret in Minneapolis.

    November 23: Opening of "Penn & Teller" at The L.A. Stage Co.

    December 13: "Thicke of the Night"—Levitation of Alan Thicke.

1984 January 8: Closing Night at the L.A. Stage Co.

    June 21–October 2: "Penn & Teller" at Dillon's in Westwood.

    October 11–October 28: "Penn & Teller" at The Whitefire Theatre in Sherman Oaks.

    December 5: Opening of Penn & Teller's return to the L.A. Stage Co. December 12: The Merv Griffin Show—Penn & Teller levitate Martin Mull.

1985 January 21: *Penn & Teller Go Public* on PBS. (Winner of 2 Emmy Awards and The International Golden Rose Award.)

    March 31: Closing night at the L.A. Stage Co.

    April 9: Opening night of "Penn & Teller" at The Westside Arts (off-Broadway) Theatre in New York City.

    May 15: "Penn & Teller" at the Westside Arts wins an Obie Award for *Whatever It Is That They Do.*

    June 26: First appearance on *Late Night with David Letterman*—The Handstab.

    September 12: Penn Jillette guest stars on the season opener of *Miami Vice.*

    September 21: *My Chauffeur*—Penn & Teller's first appearance in a movie.

    October 16: *Late Night with David Letterman*—Roaches!

    November 9: *Saturday Night Live*—The Water Tank.

    December 20: *Saturday Night Live*—The Electric Chair.

1986 February 8: *Saturday Night Live*—Upside Down Bit.

    March 21: *Saturday Night Live*—A Trick You Can Do at Home.

    April 19: *Saturday Night Live*—How to Cut a Snake in Half.

    June 16: *Late Night with David Letterman*—Rodent Roulette.

    July 1: *CBS Morning News*—Statue of Liberty Bit.

    July 21: Colin Summers becomes the P&T hacker.

    August 5: "Barbecue Death Squad from Hell."

    October 1: Guest VJs on MTV.

    October 31: MTV Halloween Party.

    November 15: *Saturday Night Live*—Casey at the Bat.

    December 13: *Saturday Night Live*—The World's Most Expensive Card Trick.

1987 January 4: Closing night at the Westside Arts.

    January 10: "Penn & Teller with the Residents" at the Warfield Theatre in San Francisco.

January 27: "It's Tricky" with Run-DMC.

February 6: *Penn & Teller's Invisible Thread* on Showtime.

February 19–22: First "Penn & Teller" show at Trump Plaza.

March 5: *Late Night with David Letterman*—Return of the Hissing Roaches.

June 9: Opening Night at Baltimore's Center Stage.

July 10: The home video of *Penn & Teller's Cruel Tricks for Dear Friends.* (Winner of the 1988 American Video Conference Award from AFI and 1989 ViRA Award.)

July 12: Closing Night at Center Stage in Baltimore.

October 31: "The Search for Houdini"—Box Escape Bit.

November 14: *Comic Relief II*—Black Art.

December 1: Opening Night of "Penn & Teller" on Broadway at The Ritz Theatre.

December 4: *The Today Show*—Scleral Shells with Jane Pauley.

December 11: *Late Night with David Letterman*—Liquid Nitrogen.

1988 February 15: Guest VJs on MTV.

    February 25: *Late Night with David Letterman*—Scleral Shells.

    March 27: Closing Night at The Ritz.

    April 1: April Fool's Day Contest on MTV.

    April 18: Principal photography starts on *Penn & Teller Get Killed.*

    June 16: Wrap date for *Penn & Teller Get Killed.*

    August 10: "Penn & Teller with The Atlanta Symphony."

    August 16–August 21: Trump Plaza.

    August 28: The Emmy Awards—Dropped washing machine on Teller.

    September 23: MTV Awards 2-hour pre-show party with Penn & Teller from Tannen's Magic Shop in NYC.

    October 9–14: Stamford Performing Arts Center.

    October 19: Opening Night of "Penn & Teller" at Boston's Colonial Theatre.

    November 13: Closing Night at the Colonial Theatre.

    November 20: Opening Night of "Penn & Teller" at San Francisco's Curran Theatre.

1989 January 15: Closing Night at the Curran Theatre.

    January 18: Opening Night of "Penn & Teller" at Philadelphia's Shubert Theatre.

    February 26: Closing Night at the Shubert.

    March 5: Pie takes over the P&T office.

    March 20: Opening Night of "Penn & Teller" at the Wiltern Theatre in Los Angeles.

    March 18: *Comic Relief III*—The Rat Cage.

    March 24: *Sonya Live in LA.*—The Dish Pan Bit.

    March 30: *Free To Be...A Family*—The National Magic Trick.

    April 16: Closing night at the Wiltern.

    April 19: Opening Night of "Penn & Teller" at Chicago's Shubert Theatre.

    May 3: *David Letterman in Chicago*—The Water Tank.

    May 28: Closing Night at The Shubert Theatre in Chicago.

    May 29: The book Penn & Teller's Cruel Tricks for Dear Friends comes out.

    June 5: Opening Night of "Penn & Teller" at Washington D.C.'s National Theatre.

    June 13: *The Today Show*—Demonstration of the book Penn & Teller's Cruel Tricks for Dear Friends for Jane Pauley.

    June 27: *Late Night with David Letterman*—The Banned Bean Chapter Bit.

    June 30: *The Larry King Show*—A special caller from Tampa named Vinnie Marengo calls in with his comments about Penn & Teller's book Cruel Tricks and Penn drops his pants on national TV.

    July 6: *CBS This Morning*—Demonstration of the book Penn & Teller's Cruel Tricks for Dear Friends for Kathleen Sullivan.

    July 9: Closing night at National Theatre.

    July 11: Penn & Teller host Showtime's *Comedy Club All-Stars III* from Caesar's Palace in Las Vegas.

    July 20: *The Search for Psychic Powers with James Randi*—The Blister Scam and Making a Car Disappear.

    August 24–27: Trump Plaza.

September 18: *After Hours*—Penn & Teller run around Times Square showing people how to *Get Killed*.

September 20: *Good Morning America*—Demonstration of the book *Penn & Teller's Cruel Tricks for Dear Friends* for Joan Londen.

September 21: *The Tonight Show with Jay Leno*—Rodent Roulette.

September 22: Opening of *Penn & Teller Get Killed*.

September 22: Penn & Teller host *Friday Night Videos*.

October 5: *The Dick Cavett Show*—Animal Traps.

October 10: *Late Night with David Letterman*—The Stigmata Bit.

October 30: *The Arsenio Hall Show*—Drill Table Clip from *Get Killed*.

1990 February 20: Robbie Libbon starts working with P&T.

February 23–February 25: Trump Plaza.

March 9 & 10: "Penn & Teller" at Caesar's Palace in Lake Tahoe.

May 8: *Late Night with David Letterman*—Sawing Teller in Half.

May 9: Release of *Penn & Teller Get Killed* on home video.

September 11: *"Live!" with Regis & Kathie Lee*—The Dish Pan Bit.

September 21: *The Today Show*—Animal Traps and Faith Daniels.

September 8–September 22: Penn & Teller practice their "Refrigerator Tour" live at SUNY Purchase.

September 25–October 14: Penn & Teller's "The Refrigerator Tour" begins in Detroit.

October 16–October 27: "The Refrigerator Tour" plays Toronto.

October 29–November 3: "The Refrigerator Tour" plays Chicago.

November 6–November 7: "The Refrigerator Tour" plays Milwaukee.

November 8: *Larry King Live*—Rodent Roulette, Bloody Hat Pin, another call from Vinnie, Teller drowns and Larry King covers his desk in plastic.

November 9–November 11: "The Refrigerator Tour" plays Baltimore.

November 16: *Late Night with David Letterman*—Dave cuts off Teller's thumb and Penn flosses his ear.

November 21–November 25: "The Refrigerator Tour" plays Minneapolis.

November 22: *The Today Show*—During satellite interview, live from Minneapolis, Penn & Teller show a clip from their special while not wearing pants.

November 23: *Penn & Teller Don't Try This at Home* airs at 8 P.M. on NBC.

November 27: *Entertainment Tonight*—Penn & Teller teach Leeza Gibbons how to cut her finger off.

November 28–December 16: "The Refrigerator Tour" plays San Francisco.

December 18–December 31: "The Refrigerator Tour" plays Los Angeles.

December 28: *Street Party with Nia Peeples* on MTV—Penn & Teller tour questionable areas of L.A.

1991 January 8: Front Page of *Personalities* TV show.

January 22–February 3: "The Refrigerator Tour" plays Philadelphia.

February 8–February 10: "The Refrigerator Tour" plays Merrillvill, IN.

February 12–February 17: "The Refrigerator Tour" plays Cleveland.

February 19–March 3: "The Refrigerator Tour" plays Boston.

February 28: Penn & Teller are inducted as honorary members of *The Harvard Lampoon*.

March 21: *Letterman*—Dish Pan and Trap.

March 26: "The Refrigerator Tour" begins performances on Broadway.

April 5: *Live At Five*—P&T call David Copperfield "Rat-Bastard."

April 10: *Good Morning America* with Charlie Gibson.

April 20: *Al Roaker's Take a Break*—Bleeding Jell-O makes TV Debut.

April 25: *Pennant Chase*—P&T & NY Knick Kiki Vandeweghe. Bean bit deemed too violent for wimpy ESPN.

April 26: *Friday Night Videos*.

April 27: Cable News Network at Sardis.

May 3: *Joan Rivers Show*—they float Joan.

May 8: *A Closer Look with Faith Daniels*—P&T don't fight with Harry Blackstone, Jr.

May 16: *"Live!" with Regis & Kathie Lee*.

May 24: *Regis and Kathie Lee*—P&T levitate Regis. Bean Trick.

June 2: Penn and Teller give themselves three Tony Awards for design. (Tony Awards steal their gag for Anthony Quinn Envelope Switch.)

June 4: Krasher takes over the Penn and Teller Office.

June 14: 3-Card-Monte Shill spits on Penn in Times Square.

June 29: "The Refrigerator Tour" closes at the O'Neill.

July 4: Penn and Teller light up ABC's *Nightline* with Independence Day Fire Eating and the 10-in-1.

July 12: *Geraldo!* An appearance by the Amazing Gordo.

July 17: Penn's turn to be Rudy on *One Life to Live*.

July 30: P&T *"Rot In Hell"* opens at the Houseman.

August 22: *Letterman*—Rathead.

September 30: P&T at Penn St.

October 6: P&T—Spielberg's Bachelor Party.

October 7: P&T at Dartmouth College.

October 20: P&T—PCCOMPUTING MVP Awards—Las Vegas.

October 28: P&T at Bowdoin College.

October 31: *"Live!" with Regis & Kathie Lee* "Halloween Jell-O."

November 15: MTV *Lip Service*—Guest Judges.

December 2: Martin Mull *Talent Takes a Holiday*.

December 20: *Letterman* "Fish"—P&T pull Dave's Breitling from the belly of a Lake Trout.

December 31: P&T host *FOX New Year's Eve LIVE!* from the Marriott Marquis, Times Square.

1992 January 19: Penn & Teller "Rot in Hell" closes at the John Houseman.

January 31: P&T at Michigan State University.

February 7: P&T at Rutgers.

April 13: P&T at Glassboro State College.

April 27: *Behind the Scenes* starts shooting.

May 7: P&T at Johnson & Wales University.

May 8, 9: P&T at the McCarter Theatre, Princeton

June 10,11: P&T: Center for the Performing Arts, San Jose.

June 12,13: P&T: Warfield Theatre, San Francisco.

June 14: P&T: Community Center Theatre, Sacramento.

August 5: Montreal—*Just for Laughs*—English Gala.

August 6: Montreal—*Just for Laughs*—Channel 4 Gala.

August 8: Montreal—*Just for Laughs*—Showtime.

August 11–16: Trump's.

September 8: *Behind the Scenes* airs.

October 9: Kirby Center, Wilkes Barre, PA.

October 10: Proctor's Theatre, Schenectady, NY.

October 11: Allentown Symphony Hall, Allentown, PA (2 Shows).

October 14: Bailey Concert Hall, Ft. Lauderdale, FL.

October 15: King Center, Melbourne, FL.

October 16: Van Wezel Perf. Arts Hall, Sarasota, FL.

October 17: Florida Theatre, Jacksonville, FL.

October 21–31: Universal Studios.

November 4: Indiana University

November 5: University of Illinois

November 6: Peoria Civic Center

November 9: NW Missouri State University

November 16: *Penn & Teller's How To Play With Your Food* in stores.